▨ Praise for EAT & Be Lean.'s Too Busy To Cook...

Seong
Working Mother

Being a working mom, the freezer meals are not only convenient, but delicious. My husband and children love to request different dishes. I suggest this book to anyone who wants to save time and still eat nutritiously.

Joel and Carolyn
Retired Couple

There are just two of us to feed each night, but we still have to eat. Freezer meals offer a great way to cook for two people without having to eat the same thing four nights in a row. We freeze the meals in portions that are just right for us. How wonderful to come home and just heat a meal up. We actually have time to wind down before dinner. "Too Busy To Cook" is a lifesaver.

David
Bachelor

Life as a bachelor is busy if not "hairy!" My mom made me single-size freezer meals to make sure I stayed alive and away from so much junk food. The variety is great and of course it costs me a lot less to pay for the groceries than to eat out. It's the only way to go!

Karen
Yours-Mine-and-Ours

I love your recipes. I just remarried and between my husband and myself we have eleven children at home. Needless to say, someone is always hungry. Thanks for making my life easier.

Paul
A Mr. Mom

In these complex times it is refreshing to find an easy-to-use program that encourages healthy, nutritious eating. The kids absolutely love these meals and they don't mind helping out.

Michelle
Student

I don't have time to fix meals most days. The demands of school and a hopefully active social life leaves little time to prepare nutritious meals. It is so fantastic to plan one Saturday to cook and know that I am eating better for the next three months without the stress. This book has probably saved my health and sanity. My only complaint is that the meals are so good that my roommates keep swiping them.

> We want to express our
> love and appreciation to our
> families and friends for their
> support, opinions, and
> patience during the
> research and development
> of this book.

Published by Thornock
International Productions, Inc.
P.O. Box 1132
Clearfield, UT
84015 • 801-776-1176

ISBN # 0 - 9629060 -7 -7

EAT &
Be Lean®

Too Busy To Cook...

By Lori L. Rogers and Chriscilla M. Thornock

- **Prepare Up To Three Months Of Meals In A Single Afternoon**

- **Low-Fat, Low-Sugar**

- **Easy, Delicious, And Still Nutritious**

- **Save Up To 20% On Grocery Bills**

Not A Meat Eater?

- These recipes can be easily converted to non-meat entrees by replacing the meat with vegetables, beans or legumes.
- Cauliflower, broccoli, carrots, corn, potatoes, kidney beans, bulgur wheat, etc., add more bulk, flavor, and healthier, unsaturated fats.
- Remember to adjust the fat grams (per portion) downward since you are using lower-fat ingredients as a substitute for meat.
- Be sure you count your fat grams and remain within the suggested 15% to 20% fat per day.

IMPORTANT NOTICE

The information contained in this book is true and complete to the best of our knowledge.   The information is meant to compliment the advice of your physician, not to replace, countermand or conflict with it. We recommend that you work with your physician in dealing with health issues and problems. Diet, exercise, mental health and medication decisions should be made between you and your health professional. Accordingly, either you or the professional treating you must take full responsibility for any use made of the information in the *Too Busy To Cook* book. The authors and publisher disclaim all liability in connection with the use of this book.

Sorry about this disclaimer, but the attorneys made us do it!

Table of Contents

3 tsp.	1 Tbl.
4 Tbl.	1/4 cup
5 1/3 Tbl.	1/3 cup
8 Tbl.	1/2 cup
10 2/3 Tbl.	2/3 cup
12 Tbl.	3/4 cup
16 Tbl.	1 cup
1/2 cup	1 gill
2 cups	1 pt.
4 cups	1 qt.
4 qts.	1 gal.
8 qts.	1 peck
4 pecks	1 bu.
16 oz.	1 lb.
32 oz.	1 qt.
8 oz. liquid	1 cup
1 oz. liquid	2 Tbl.

For liquid and dry measurements use standard measuring spoon and cups.
All measurements are level.

WEIGHTS AND MEASURES

Baking Powder
1 cup = 5 1/2 oz.

Brown Sugar
1 lb. brown = 2 1/2 cups

Butter
1 lb. = 2 cups

Cheese
1 lb. = 2 2/3 cups cubed
1 lb. = 4 cups grated

Corn Meal
1 lb. = 3 cups

Eggs
1 egg = 4 Tbl. liquid
4 to 5 whole = 1 cup
7 to 9 whites = 1 cup
12 to 14 yolks = 1 cup

Flour
1 lb. = 4 cups

Gelatin
1/4 oz. pkg. unflavored = 1 Tbl.

Lemons, Juice
1 medium = 2 to 3 Tbl.
5 to 8 medium = 1 cup

Lemon, Rind
1 lemon = 1 Tbl. grated

Oranges, Juice
1 medium = 2 to 3 Tbl.
3 to 4 medium = 1 cup

Oranges, Rind
1 = 2 Tbl. grated

Charts

7

Lean Hamburger

 =

1 Pound

Approximately
2 cups cooked

Boneless, Skinless Chicken Breast

 =

1 Pound

Approximately
3 cups cooked,
broken up

Chicken Breast

 =

1 Single
(1/2 side of
whole breast)

Approximately
1 cup cooked

Onion

 =

1 Large

Approximately
1 cup chopped

Green Pepper

 =

1 Large

Approximately
1 cup chopped

Cheese

 =

1 Pound

Approximately
4 cups grated

Carrots

 =

2 medium

Approximately
1 cup shredded

Celery

 =

2 single
stalks
from
bunch

Approximately
1 cup chopped

INTRODUCTION

EAT & Be Lean. is a life-style of healthier, low-fat, low-sugar eating that has helped people all over the world become permanently lean, healthy and energetic. The simple principles taught in the EAT & Be Lean *SUCCESS FORMULA* manual are easy to understand and implement for the entire family and will be of value to you as you desire more in-depth information.

Whether you are new to EAT & Be Lean., or a graduate already utilizing the educational program found in the *SUCCESS FORMULA* manual and nine week audio course, we are excited to introduce you to our version of *fast foods* without the problem of added harmful drugs, chemicals, and depleted nutrition. We don't recommend every meal be a freezer meal because there is some nutritional loss in the process. You will find these meals to be delicious, healthy, convenient, and a terrific alternative to processed or junk food.

Use as many fresh fruits, grains, and vegetables as possible when you are cooking. The process used in preparing foods will determine their nutritional value. Since fresh, raw veggies, grains, and fruits contain the highest nutritional value, you should use plenty of them as side dishes along with your frozen entree.

Though we have used some canned foods in our recipes, you should be aware that we use as few as possible because canned foods are nutritionally empty foods and usually have high sodium content. We heartily encourage the use of homemade soups, sauces, etc. made from fresh ingredients as substitutions in these recipes.

We are very pleased to share these cooking and freezing techniques that provide easy, tasty, successful meals to get you started on your own journey of healthy and convenient eating.

Sincerely,

Lori L. Rogers

Chriscilla M. Thornock   and   O. Van Thornock
THORNOCK INTERNATIONAL PRODUCTIONS, Inc.

INTRODUCTION

This cookbook is the busy person's answer to cooking quick meals without sacrificing total nutrition or taste. There is no limit to the variety of meals you can have when you learn to take your own favorite family recipes, or any recipe for that matter, and make them into freezer meals. Even a four year old child can be taught how to prepare a balanced meal using the freezer meals. These cooking techniques are simple to perform and the meals are delicious to eat.

This book is for you, whether you are a:

1. bachelor or bachelorette on the move.
2. student with limited time.
3. busy mother who must carefully calculate every waking moment.
4. single parent who does it all.
5. elderly couple who's just plain tired of cooking and eating out.
6. concerned son or daughter whose parents need help, but want to maintain their independence.
7. friend taking in a meal to help a sick neighbor.
8. child who needs to prepare meals because both parents work.
9. working mom.
10. person who just simply hates to cook.

These techniques are a pleasant alternative to spending hours in the kitchen, every day of your life. The time you do spend will be very efficient, and the time required to prepare your menus will be reduced as you sharpen your ability to use these techniques.

■■■■■ HOW DOES IT WORK?

Have you ever made a double batch of lasagna and then frozen one for later? Perhaps you have doubled your chili recipe so you wouldn't have to go through all the hassle again later? Well, take that idea and expand it several times over and you have what we call the "Too Busy To Cook" approach to cooking. With this plan, you make all the mess and get all of the hassle over with all at once. It makes a lot of sense to grate the entire block of cheese while you have the grater out rather than just a little, or chop four onions rather than 1/4 cup. The clean-up is still the same and it doesn't take much longer either.

Don't panic at the thought of a marathon cooking day. If there are two people to help, it can be done. There are simple ways to do it. Select your day of cooking, or split up the days if you wish. We recommend dividing up the cooking into two or three short days. Do what fits your schedule best.

This is how it works:

ONE DAY OR TWO AFTERNOONS TO FREEDOM			
STEPS		**TIME**	**TASK**
1 Day 1		5 minutes	Decide on the meals you want for the month (select 10 to 20 different recipes).
2		25 minutes	Make a shopping list.
3		90 minutes	Go shopping.
4	Day 1	10 minutes	Separate goods on counter into categories.
5		10 minutes	Set out cooking equipment.
6		10 minutes	Start your meats cooking.
7		10 minutes	Grate all of the cheeses. Check meats.
8		30 minutes	Wash / cut up fruits and veggies. Check meats.
9		20 minutes	Label the freezer bags with directions.
10	Day 2	120 minutes	Make up freezer meals, seal and freeze.
11		30 minutes	Clean up kitchen. SIMPLE!

THREE SHORT AFTERNOONS TO FREEDOM

STEP	TIME	TASK
Tuesday 2 Hours Total	5 minutes	Decide on the meals you want for the month (select 10 to 20 different recipes).
	25 minutes	Make a shopping list.
	90 minutes	Go shopping.
Wednesday 1 Hour 10 Min.	10 minutes	Separate goods on counter into categories.
	10 minutes	Set out cooking equipment.
	10 minutes	Start your meats cooking.
	10 minutes	Grate all of the cheeses. Check meats.
	30 minutes	Wash/cut up fruits/veggies. Refrigerate. Clean-up
Thursday 2 Hours 50 Min.	20 minutes	Label freezer bags with directions.
	120 minutes	Make up freezer meals, seal and freeze.
	30 minutes	Clean up kitchen. SIMPLE!

When it comes time to enjoy the dinners, most meals can be reheated in the microwave. Also, conventional oven features such as *time-bake* can really simplify and cut down meal preparation time. You can place dinner (other than chicken or turkey) in a baking dish earlier in the day to thaw. The automatic time-bake feature can be pre-programed to start before you get home. You arrive home to the wonderful smells of your dinner already cooked, hot, and ready to eat.

IMAGINE THE BENEFITS
From Mealtime Madness To Fun and Games

Normally, meal time is a panic. If you're a working mother or single parent, the moment you get home, you frantically try to think of something to eat and prepare it while trying to entertain the troops as they wait impatiently for dinner. Hungry kids can create a high-stress atmosphere to say the least. By the time you sit down to eat, you're beat! How can you

possibly enjoy dinner with the upset you've just experienced. After that, you have to face the cleanup nightmare. Yuk!

Wouldn't it be nice to have the chance to sit and talk with your spouse, read the newspaper, or play games with the kids while the nutritious meal you've chosen is cooking. Cleanup is just as relaxed since there aren't several pots, bowls and utensils lying around from the cooking process. Other than the dinnerware, you probably have one bowl or pot to clean, and that may even be the one you served it in. Mealtime madness turns into a relaxed time for association with your family or friends. Just think of the stress reduction that takes place in this situation. You'll probably be more pleasant to be with for the rest of the evening. What a benefit to your sanity, not to mention everyone else's.

The 26 Hour Day

Every day, for 365 days per year, you will spend one to two hours per day preparing an evening meal. That averages anywhere between 365 and 730 hours per year that you must set aside to cook for your growling stomach or growling family, at the end of a long, tiring day. Wouldn't you rather spend six to eight hours a month or maybe only every three months cooking those evening meals instead? Here at EAT & Be Lean® we would, and we do! For a single person, married couple, or a small family that may add up to only 24 hours (4 days) of cooking per year. For a family of 6 or more it may be only 72 hours (or 12 days) of cooking for the entire year. WOW! This technique could eliminate 80-97% of your time spent in the kitchen for the year. Who wouldn't want an extra free hour or two a day, 658 free hours a year? It's like having 26 hours in each day. The thought is exciting! You'll still want to cook to some extent each week, but you'll enjoy it rather than dread it!

A Penny Saved Is A Penny Earned

Freezer meals can save you hundreds of dollars over a period of a year. It's easy to see why.

1. You buy what you need instead of buying what sounds good today and terrible tomorrow. Foods bought without planning first generally end up sitting in the cupboard or refrigerator and spoiling, rotting, or drying out before you use them. A lot of money goes down the drain that way.

2. It discourages impulse shopping when you are hungry. Have you ever noticed how you go for the fast foods that contain a higher sugar and fat content when you shop hungry? Processed and prepackaged foods cost more, contain harmful chemicals and preservatives, and are far less nutritious.

3. You use what you buy with very few, if any, leftovers. No waste equals greater savings.

4. You make fewer trips to the market, saving gas money and valuable time.

5. You can stock up when items you use frequently go on sale. For example, boneless-skinless chicken is usually expensive, but when it goes on sale it's good to buy as much as possible. You can freeze items like that and have them available at a later date for a much lower price.

6. When you know what items you purchase frequently, you can buy on case lot sales in bulk (creating a good food storage situation) saving you a considerable amount of money in the long run.

By preparing freezer meals, you can cut down your monthly grocery costs by one third to one half. The degree of savings depends upon your prior eating and shopping habits. You will still need to go to the store for breakfast items and lunch items to an extent, but you can go when you have time and even possibly enjoy it.

Total Class Act

Men, women, and children can get in on the act. Anyone can be taught how to prepare a balanced meal with very little effort. Even husbands and young children can learn and help. If you are old enough to read and follow simple instructions, you can prepare a freezer meal dinner that looks and tastes like you've spent all day working at it. That means everyone can relax and contribute, making dinner time the most special time of the day to be together. For example: One night you are late getting home and even though you have a meal ready to go in the oven, you aren't there to put it in. You know dinner is going to be late for sure. But, since baking directions are printed on the freezer bag, your husband, or roommate, or even one of the kids can put dinner in the oven for you. When you get home, you can make a fresh vegetable salad in 10 minutes, cut up some fresh fruit in five minutes, and put some whole wheat rolls on the table for a completely balanced, delicious meal in a grand total of 15 minutes. You can still eat on time, and dinner-time frustration will be a thing of the past!

Spacing Out?

When you shop on a daily or weekly basis, running out of refrigerator and freezer space is an automatic outcome. The space saving benefits of doing freezer meals is incredible. It's really easy to stack 20 to 25 meals (one gallon size bags) in a normal freezer above your refrigerator. You can stack an additional 30 to

35 single-meal-size bags (for quick lunches) along the edges and in the nooks and crannies that remain. That's easily one month's worth of meals for a family of six to eight people. If you are single, there's just the two of you, or you have a small family of four to five, you could stack three months worth of meals in the smaller quart-size bag.

LET'S GET COOKIN'

There are a few differences in techniques depending upon the number of people you are cooking for. Cooking for one is as easy as cooking for six, but there are a few tricks that you'll need to understand. The tricks are logical and will be easy to implement, so don't fret.

Cooking for One or Two People

Recipes are designed to feed a larger amount of people. Since you are only cooking for one or two, you are able to increase the reward without increasing the effort.

1. Use single serving (pint size), zipper freezer bags.
2. Do only half as many recipes and divide them into three or four meals. For example, ten recipes will make 30 to 40 meals. Double the pleasure, but not double the work!

That's how you can get up to three months worth of meals.

Cooking For A Small Family

Most of the meals in this book will feed a family of at least six. If your family is smaller than six, we still suggest you make the whole recipe, divide it evenly, and freeze the food in two quart-size bags. (A few recipes, such as enchiladas, may still require a gallon size bag.)

When you make 20 recipes, you

actually get 40 meals. You can stretch those 40 meals out to last about three months since you'll only eat a freezer meal three to four times a week. The other days you can wing it. You might go out once, snack on Saturday night, eat a roast on Sunday, or just fill in. Sometimes pancakes are nice for dinner!

Cooking For A Large Family

If you have a family or group larger than six to eight people, double the recipes, double the freezer bags and continue with the same procedure as for the smaller families.

If it makes the meals too big for your needs, you might try doubling the recipe and then dividing it into three bags. Whatever works for you.

Converting Favorite Family Recipes

You probably have many recipes that your family enjoys. You can easily use many of these recipes as your own freezer meals. Refer to the front of the book for equivalency charts that will help in converting your recipes. You will discover many things for yourself through experience. In this book, there are helpful hints that will assist you in choosing which of your recipes can be frozen, and which things do not freeze well. One thing that is a good idea to do, until you feel a little more comfortable about how to freeze foods, is to make a meal that your family likes for dinner, then freeze a single portion in a pint-size freezer bag. Let it stay frozen for at least three weeks. Then heat it up and see how it tastes. This way you will know whether you need to add more liquid (maybe it's too dry), take liquid out (maybe it's too soggy), or whatever, next time you freeze it. Making the necessary improvements will come easy to you with time. Be patient and enjoy the learning process. You *will* get it!

REDUCING THE FAT

Judging by the success of the fast food industry, it is obvious that people want fast, easy meals. Besides the expense, the problem with most fast foods is that they are loaded with chemicals and preservatives, and are dripping with fat! It is easy to get over 65 grams of fat in one fast food meal. Take the "s" out of fast, and you have what most of them are, "Fat Foods." Considering that an average woman should eat approximately 1800 to 2000 calories a day, and it is recommended that only about 20% of those calories be from fat, the average woman should only have between 30 and 46 grams of fat per day, not 65 grams per meal!

The recipes included in this book have reduced amounts of cheese and meat or have substituted ingredients for high-fat ingredients. You can lower the fat in much of your own cooking by using some of the following simple hints:

General Healthification Tips

- Remember, cholesterol-free doesn't necessarily mean fat-free. Look for things low in fat, not just low in cholesterol.

- Don't be as concerned with calories as you are with FAT. Calories themselves aren't bad. It's the *high saturated fat intake and altered fat* calories that are the culprits.

- Cut down the amount of cheese and meat in recipes. These are used for flavor and texture, and you can get that with about half as much cheese or meat and really cut down on fat.

- Eat when you are hungry. By eating complex (not refined) carbohydrate calories and moderate amounts of essential fat calories, you will speed up your metabolism. Healthy snacks such as veggies, grains and fruits *are good* for you.

- Watch out for items that say "lite" or "diet". That doesn't necessarily mean lower in fat. Check the fat grams verses the calories per serving.

- Avoid artificial sweeteners. They can cause brain damage in everyone who uses them, including unborn babies.

- Avoid foods containing monosodium glutamate (MSG). MSG does not change the taste of food. It is a drug and is a stress to the body. It activates your taste buds and fools the brain into thinking that the food tastes more flavorful. Poor quality products are enhanced by this drug and therefore sold more frequently at a cheaper cost to the manufacturer. It can also have harmful effects on some people.

- Use lite salt.

Grains

- Use whole grain products rather than processed, stripped, refined foods. Avoid products using "enriched" flour. It's a tricky way of trying to make you believe that what you are getting is healthy.

- Mix bulgur wheat with red meats to add bulk without fat. The taste remains the same, but it is much healthier.

Gravy

- Get the fat off of the broth before making gravy. To do this, empty a tray of ice cubes into the broth. (Don't stir, this just melts the ice.) Let the fat harden, then simply remove with a spoon. You can also chill the broth in the refrigerator, then skim the hardened fat off of the top.

- Make cornstarch gravies or use ULTRA GEL® which is a modified cornstarch that thickens in hot or cold temperatures.

Meats

- Use tuna packed in water, **not** oil.
- Use LEAN or EXTRA LEAN ground beef.

- Cook hamburger in a pan that is tilted to allow the fat to run off of the meat as it is cooked. Drain hamburger in a colander and rinse with hot water to get rid of most of the fat.

- Bake, broil, or boil instead of frying when possible.

- Buy chicken breasts instead of whole chickens. Breasts contain only white meat, which is lower in fat. If possible, it's most convenient to buy skinless, boneless chicken breasts to begin with.

- If you do use a whole chicken, skin it *before* cooking. Most of the fat is in the skin. A whole chicken has 2000 calories. 1200 of those calories are found in the skin in the form of fat. 600 of the 1200 fat calories absorb into the meat if you cook the chicken before skinning it.

- Dip chicken in fat-free Italian dressing instead of beaten egg when coating with bread crumbs.

- Substitute egg whites for egg yolks or whole eggs. Two whites equal one whole egg.

Spreads

- Use Molly McButter® or Butter Buds® rather than butter or margarine. Choose real butter over margarine as a second choice.

- Always remember, though butter is supposedly higher in fat than margarine, *butter is better*! Margarine contains up to 47% trans fats (altered fats) which are very harmful to the body. Use "real" butter, but be "real" moderate.

- If you use reduced-fat or fat-free mayonnaise and salad dressings, do so with the understanding that you are receiving added preservatives and chemicals from these products. This is trading the problem of excess fat in regular

mayonnaise and salad dressing for the problem of added chemicals. Maybe cutting down on the regular, high-fat product would be a healthier choice. Nevertheless, the choice is yours to make.

Dairy

- Use fat-free or at least low-fat dairy products.

- Use skim in place of 1%, 2% or whole milk. In cooking, the difference in taste is little, and the difference in fat is incredible! Be aware that homogenized, pasteurized milk can be damaging to your body because of the modified fats. The less you use the better. Look for your own favorite substitutes and consider learning how to make and use nut or soy milks.

- Part skim Mozzarella cheese has almost half the fat of cheddar. Use more Mozzarella! You can also use reduced-fat cheeses in your recipes. Real Parmesan cheese is a good choice because of the strong flavor. You use less cheese to obtain the same amount of flavor, but eat less fat in the process.

- Substitute nonfat sour cream or plain yogurt in recipes.

Oils

- Cut down on oil in recipes. If the recipe says fry in 1/4 cup of oil, you can generally use a couple of tablespoons instead, depending upon the recipe.

- Use cooking sprays instead of oil or shortening for cooking and baking.

- Use cold pressed olive or Canola oil and adjust the amount used in your homemade recipes. You can cut it down considerably! (Try half as much.)

- Mashed fruit such as applesauce can replace oil in cookies, muffins, cakes and breads. It's a wonderful substitution.

- Try increasing the water to take the place of oil in cake mixes. If the mix calls for one cup of water and 1/3 cup of oil, use 1 1/3 cups of water and no oil. You'll be surprised at how good it tastes. (Cake mixes already contain some shortening.)

QUICK REFERENCE - FREEZING TECHNIQUES

ITEM / PROBLEM	SOLUTION
POTATOES • Turn soggy when frozen • Too much moisture	• Use Ore-Ida frozen potato hashbrowns.
CHEESE, HARD • Crumbles if frozen whole.	• Grate it first, mix in a small amount of cornstarch to prevent clumping.
WHITE SAUCE • Generally doesn't freeze well. Curdles and/or separates when reheated.	• Use ULTRA GEL® or Clear Gel to thicken sauce. Health food stores may have these or see the product order form in back of book.
MEATS • **Never thaw and refreeze** meats without cooking first. Harmful bacteria will develop in the process.	• When preparing meat loaf, buy fresh lean ground meat to make it instead of thawing some you might have in the freezer.
RICE AND PASTA • Fully cooked rice and pastas can turn mushy when thawed and re-cooked.	• *Slightly* under-cook rice and pasta in meals you plan to freeze. They will finish cooking when heated through.
BULGUR WHEAT • Too crunchy in foods.	• Crack it in a food processor or blender and boil it for 5 to 10 minutes before using.
SOGGY FOOD • Entree is soggy after reheating.	• Reduce liquids in recipe, 1/4 cup at a time.

HELPFUL FREEZING HINTS

Pre-Cooling Foods

- Cool foods on the counter or in the fridge for 30 minutes before freezing them. Adding hot foods to a freezer, especially a small one, will raise the temperature inside and overwork your freezer. Ice cream, orange juice, etc. may melt.

Labeling

- Be sure to label and date your meals with a permanent marker. It really can be hard to tell what the entree is when it's frozen. Write baking directions on the bag so you don't have to use a cookbook to heat the meal.

Freezers

- If you have a small freezer, quick-freeze the meals on a cookie sheet first so they lay perfectly flat. They are a lot easier to store and save a lot more space if they are flat.

- In a freezer kept at 0 degrees Fahrenheit (a "deep-freeze"), you can keep meals for two or three months. In a freezer that is attached to your refrigerator, meals will last for about one month.

Baking Time

- Increase baking time and/or temperature slightly when you bake your own recipes. When foods are cold (even if they are thawed) they take longer to cook.

Liquid

- In some of your own recipes you may have to cut back by as much as 1/2 cup liquid or they may become soggy.

 Generally speaking, however, if you have rice or noodles in a meal, don't cut back on the liquid.

Maintaining the Flavor

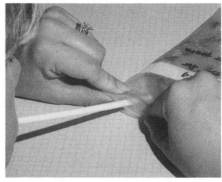

- Remove as much air as possible from the freezer bag (fig.1). You can either zip the bag most of the way and suck the rest of the air out with a straw, or set the bag on the counter, fold the top over, push the air out, then seal it. Air in the bag

Figure 1 - Removing the air.

allows ice crystals to form on the food, which can make it taste soggy, or give it a "freezer taste."

Extraction Problems? (Getting The Food Out!)

- With some meals you may have to cut the bag open to get the meal out in one piece. Go ahead--get the scissors! Lift the enchiladas, for instance, out with your hands and put them into the pan you are going to bake them in.

- Spray all of your baking dishes with a cooking spray (such as PAM) before cooking -- then the contents won't stick.

GETTING STARTED

To help you get started, ten delicious easy freezer meals have been chosen for you. The recipes and shopping list are also provided for you. We suggest you start out with ten and expand as you feel more comfortable. (Preparing 20 meals at a time becomes a snap with a little practice.) The preparation process will be explained, and it should take you only two to three hours to prepare the meals. You will have two weeks of hassle-free dinners for a large family, or a month's worth of dinners for a small family! All you have to do is shop, prepare, freeze, and eat!

Here are the ten meals that we have found to be easy, quick, and perfect for you to experience how simple this technique really is. Stay calm and have fun through this learning process. The first time is always the hardest, but you'll see that even at it's hardest it's pretty easy.

■ 1st Ten Freezer Meals

Everything for these ten meals has been included on the shopping list located on the following pages. Put <u>everything</u> on the list so you don't have to go through the recipes and check to see if you might be missing something. It's easier to just look down the list and cross off the things you already have.

Let's learn how to shop!

* Fat FREE
** No MSG ®

1st Ten Freezer Meals

M E A L S		
	1	Chicken Divan
	2	Chicken Enchiladas
	3	Chicken Fajitas
	4	Chinese Sundaes
	5	Lasagna

VEGETABLES AND FRUITS

ITEM	SIZE / AMOUNT	# USED IN RECIPE	TOTAL	PRICE	Actual Cost For Amount Used
onion	medium	𝍩𝍩 11	7	2.07	2.07
green pepper	medium	11	2	.66	.66
zucchini	medium	1/2 cup	1	.79	.79
carrots	medium	1 cup	2	.20	.20
tomatoes	medium	111	3	.99	.99
celery	bunch	2 cups	1	.68	.68
green onions	bunch	2 cups	1	.33	.33
red pepper	medium	1	1	.98	.98

DRYFOODS

brown rice (16 oz. bag)	cups	𝍩𝍩𝍩 11	2 bags	1.38	1.38
Old El Paso taco seasoning mix**	1 pkg.	1	1 pkg.	.69	.69
wheat (to make bulgur wheat)	cups	111	1 bag	2.53	.60
whole wheat lasagna noodles	8 oz.	1	1 box	1.69	1.69
whole wheat hamburger buns	pkg. - 12	1	1 pkg.	1.98	1.98
corn taco shells	pkg. - 12	1	1 pkg.	.95	.95
whole wheat bread	loaf	1	1 pkg.	1.25	1.25
picante sauce	16 oz.	10 oz.	1 btl.	1.59	1.59
Worcestershire Sauce	5 oz. btl.	1	1	.85	.17
taco sauce	cup	1/2 cup	16 oz.	1.39	.34

SPICES

basil, cumin, oregano			3		
ULTRA GEL® or cornstarch,	**These are infrequent**		1		Appx.
parsley flakes, chili powder,	**purchases and become**		2		$1.50
garlic powder, curry, salt,	**kitchen staples...**		3		total
pepper, paprika			2		

MEATS

turkey bacon	1 pkg.	1	1	1.89	.40
ground beef	cup	𝍩	3 lbs.	4.58	4.58
boneless skinless chicken breast	cups	𝍩𝍩𝍩𝍩 1111	31/2 lbs.	6.97	6.97

Equivalents: 1 lb. hamburger = 16 oz. = appx. 3 cups chunked
1 lb. boneless, skinless chicken = 16 oz. = appx. 2 1/2 cups chopped
1 boneless, skinless chicken breast = appx. 1 cup chopped
1 large onion = appx. 1 cup chopped

Shopping Planner

CANNED FOODS

ITEM	SIZE / AMOUNT	# USED IN RECIPE	TOTAL	PRICE	Actual Cost For Amount Used
tomato sauce	8 oz.	111	24 oz.	.99	.99
cream of chicken soup**	10 3/4 oz.	111	3	2.85	2.85
cream or mushroom soup**	10 3/4 oz.	1	1	.89	.89
Campbell's Spaghetti Sauce	26 1/2 oz.	1	1	1.03	1.03
ketchup	14 oz.	1	1	.89	.23
kidney beans	can	1	1	.57	.57
vegetarian refried beans	can	1	1	.69	.69
lemon juice	7.5 oz.	1	1	1.39	.08
mushrooms	4 oz.	1	1	.69	.69
chicken broth**	8 oz.	111	3	2.61	2.61
chicken gumbo soup**	10 3/4 oz.	1	1 can	.69	.69
mustard	Tbl.	1/2	sm. btl.	.59	.03
green chilies	4 oz.	1	1 can	.49	.49

FROZEN FOODS

frozen corn	16 oz. pkg.	1	1	.87	.87
frozen hashbrowns	32 oz. pkg.	1	1	.69	.69
frozen chopped broccoli	16 oz. pkg.	1	1	1.19	1.19
green beans, fresh frozen	8 oz. bag	1	1	.35	.35

DAIRY SECTION

skim milk	cups	1/2 cup	1/2 gal.	1.22	.03
cheddar cheese	cups	1 1	18 oz.	2.59	2.59
nonfat cottage cheese*	16 oz.	1	1	1.79	1.79
nonfat ricotta cheese*	16 oz.	1	1 carton	2.39	2.39
Parmesan cheese, fresh	cups	1/3 cup	4 oz.	1.89	.95
skim mozarella cheese(Frigo Truly Lite)	cups	1 1/3 cups	12 oz.	4.79	4.79
whole wheat tortilla (1 fat gram ea.)	pkg. - 10	10 tortillas	1 pkg.	1.69	1.69
yogurt - plain nonfat	4 oz.	1	1 cntr.	1.19	1.19
soft corn tortillas	pkg. - 12	1	1	.45	.45
fat free sour cream*	cups	1/2 cup	8 oz.	1.39	.70

	Subtotal	**62.27**
	6.25% Sales Tax	3.89
	Total $	66.16

Note: These ten freezer meals create 98 individual entrees. Total cost per entree would be 68 cents each. **No waste!**

SHOPPING - STEP 1

As shown prior, categorize your shopping list as follows:

1. Dairy Products
2. Canned and Bottled Foods
3. Dry Foods
4. Produce
5. Meats
6. Frozen Foods

There are two reasons for this. First, if your list is categorized, it's easy to write down the things you need and add to your list with each new recipe. Second, it helps to save time when you actually go shopping because you can get all of your produce while you are in the produce section, etc., without zigzagging and backtracking all around the store.

Remember to include your favorite vegetables, salad fixings, breads, etc. to go with your meals. These will be an important source of live vitamins and enzymes at full strength and are essential additions with frozen entree's. Also, remember to add breakfast and lunch foods, snacks, condiments and staples, cleaning supplies, soaps, drinks, desserts, and extra things your family needs. Freezer meals are super, but if you have no food for breakfast and lunch, you still have to go back to the store. Now, as necessary, add to the shopping list located on the previous page and go shopping.

PREPARATION INSTRUCTIONS - STEP 2

Begin by obtaining and organizing all of the ingredients. Whether you're doing your meals alone or with help, this preparatory work will make assembly of the meals a lot easier.

▨▨▨ Groceries

When you get home from shopping, refrigerate perishables and leave everything else out on the counter. If you put it away, you will have to search for it when you're ready to use it, and that wastes time!

▨▨▨ Hamburger and Chicken

Brown all of the ground beef and boil all of the chicken.

A. Locate a broiling pan that will allow the grease to drain off as it cooks. Break up the ground beef and place it in the pan. Cover the meat loosely with aluminum foil and put it in the oven at about 400°. Rearrange the meat about every 20 minutes.

B. While your hamburger is baking, put the boneless skinless chicken breasts (boneless, skinless is what we recommend -- it saves a lot of time) in a big roasting pan, cover with water, and put on high heat. Leave the pan uncovered. When the water starts to boil, turn the heat down to medium so it doesn't boil over.

The chicken and hamburger will take approximately 30 to 60 minutes to cook. Make sure that there are no pink parts in the meat.

▨▨▨ Vegetables and Cheese

While the hamburger is baking and the chicken is boiling, you can begin chopping or slicing the vegetables and grating the cheeses. A food processor is a lifesaver in this step. (You can get one that is very adequate for about $30 and it is well worth the investment.) First slice the carrots, then chop the onions. Next, chop the green peppers by hand because the food processor

will not chop it well! Put the vegetables in separate bowls, cover, and refrigerate. The rest of the vegetables are for the Chinese Sundaes and will be used when you eat that meal. If you pre-chop the vegetables for the Chinese Sundaes along with all of the others, make sure you use this frozen entree early in the first week. Your vegetables will be fresh if you'll do this and yield greater nutritional value. Next, grate the mozzarella cheese, put it into a bowl, cover, and place in the refrigerator-then do the same with the cheddar cheese.

Back to the Hamburger and Chicken

When the chicken is done, drain the water off, rinse in cold water to cool, and break into bite-size pieces. When the hamburger is fully cooked, take it out of the oven, place a colander inside a large bowl and rinse the hamburger in hot water. Then take the chunks and, using the chopper blade of the food processor, pulse the machine on and off to chop the chunks of hamburger into nice pieces that are ready to go into your meals. Be careful not to over-chop. Cover both the hamburger and chicken and put them in the fridge until you are ready to make your meals. The food will be fine as long as it is covered and in the refrigerator.

Call It A Day

Congratulations! You've just completed the "preparatory work." Pretty easy, don't you think? You can call it a day right now, and finish the rest tomorrow, or keep going.

When you do more than ten meals, you probably won't want to complete it all in one day. Split it up into two, or even three days. You can do the preparatory work (as explained above) on the first day, assemble the hamburger meals on the second day, and the chicken meals on the third day. These particular ten meals will go so fast you can probably do them all at once.

ASSEMBLY INSTRUCTIONS - STEP 3

Now, you're ready to assemble the meals. Start with all of your hamburger recipes. Put the **Spanish Rice Casserole** together first. Cook the four turkey-bacon strips in the microwave between two paper towels. While these are cooking (approximately 5-8 minutes), combine the rest of the ingredients. When the bacon is crispy, crumble it up and add it to the rest of the ingredients.

Next, do the **Sloppy Joes, Shepherd's Pie, Tostadas**, and finally the traditional **Lasagna**. All of the hamburger meals are done. You can either do the chicken now, or wait until tomorrow.

Start the chicken meals with the **Chicken Fajitas**. Put them together, label the bag, remove air, and freeze. Next, put the **Chicken Divan** together. Both of these meals are simple and should go really fast. After these are done, do the **Mexican Chicken**. Next comes the **Chinese Sundaes**, and finally the **Chicken Enchiladas**.

Way To Go! You have just completed ten recipes in record time. But don't be fooled, next time it will go even faster.

You will have some items left over when you cook these ten meals. You will use them later as you eat the meals. You should have used everything <u>except</u>: lettuce, tomatoes, taco shells for the tostadas, some green pepper, celery, pineapple tidbits, green onion, grated cheese for the Chinese Sundaes, tortillafor the Chicken Fajitas, and hamburger buns for the Sloppy Joes. Though regular brown rice is best to use because it is more nutritious, brown *minute* rice may be used when your time is *really* short and you need rice for meals such as Chinese Sundaes. Plan accordingly when preparing your shopping list.

Labeling and Freezing

Remember to label and date all the bags with a permanent marker (Fig. 2). Then include baking directions so you don't have to look up the recipe to see how to bake it. (Do this before you fill the bag. The writing is much easier!)

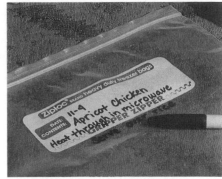

Figure 2 - Labeling the bag.

Put the meal into a gallon-size bag (see fig. 3, page 33) for a large family, or divide evenly and put into two quart-size bags for a small family. Remove the air by zipping the bag most of the way shut, inserting a straw, and sucking the air out of the bag. Then pinch that opening closed, finish sealing the bag, and almost all of the air should be out! Your entree is ready to freeze!

Quick Thawing Instructions

Thawing is easy. Remove the meal bag from the freezer and place it in a sink full of hot water. Allow approximately 20 to 30 minutes to thaw. Immediately bake your thawed meal. See also, "Using Ovens and Microwaves" below.

Using Ovens and Microwaves

Due to differences in ovens, and how thawed a meal is, the baking times given in the following recipes are guidelines (pretty close, but maybe not exact). You may have to adjust for your own oven or circumstances. Be flexible!

Most of the meals in this book can be reheated in the microwave. However, if the meal has raw rice or dry noodles, it will definitely need to be cooked in the oven so they will have time to get done. Using the conventional oven has the added convenience of the time-bake option.

It gives a certain crispiness to some meals -- microwaves sometimes have the tendency to make things soggy. However, if you feel comfortable using your microwave, go ahead!

General Guidelines

Unless specifically stated **RAW**, all the recipes in this book use **cooked** meat. This is one of the features that makes "Meal Making" so great. With all the meat cooked at once, all you have to do is measure it for the recipe. The recipes also call for meat and vegetables in cups, rather than pounds, which makes it faster and easier to make all your meals at once.

Necessary Equipment

Figure 3 - Filling Freezer Bags: Place gallon bag in two quart pitcher or quart bag in 32 ounce cup.

- Cook book
- Measuring spoons and cups
- 1 gallon-size freezer bags
- quart-size freezer bags
- 2 large holding bowls
- 5 small - medium holding bowls
- 1 large mixing bowl
- Food processor
- 1 large boiling pot
- 1 broiling pan
- two-quart pitcher
- 32 oz. cup
- 2 - 9"x13" baking dishes
- 2 - 8"x 8" baking dishes
- Permanent bullet point marker
- Can opener
- Colander
- 1 large spoon
- 1 fork
- Hot pads
- Straw

READY FOR MORE?

Once you have made the ten easy recipes, you can go on to a little more complicated recipes. Don't panic! They aren't that hard--and it won't take much longer than the first ten. On the following page you will find ten more recipe suggestions. Practice setting up the shopping list for them on pages 36 and 37 and then go shopping. Later, when you get really brave, combine the two and make twenty using the shopping list on pages 90 and 91.

2nd Ten Freezer Meals

Once again, mark off the items on the shopping list that you already have at home so you won't be duplicating products. You may even have some of the necessary items left over from the first shopping list.

Prepare these meals as per the instructions given on the first ten meals. You can do it--you'll do fine!

RUNNING ON YOUR OWN

Now that you have completed the process once, it is easy to see why it is such a great idea. The first thing you need to do is decide what recipes you are going to use. Look through the index and make a list. Solicit everyone's help when you do this. Let everyone choose their five favorite meals, and you won't have to decide what you're going to have all by yourself.

After the meals are chosen, the next step is to make up a shopping list, combining the common ingredients so you can buy in bulk. Go through your recipes and check <u>all</u> the ingredients as you are making your list so you don't forget staples that may be running low, and then go shopping.

■■■■USING OTHER COOKBOOKS

We've suggested a few meals from the **EAT** & Be Lean®
SUCCESS FORMULA manual and **FAVORITE FAMILY
RECIPES** cookbook that work well with the freezing techniques
you've just learned. This will get you started. You'll see how
easy it is to use other recipes as time goes on and how easy it
is to identify which ones will work and which ones won't.

These are only a few of the recipes that will work. Try
them after you've done the process once or twice.

2nd Ten Freezer Meals

* Fat FREE
** No MSG ®

VEGETABLES AND FRUITS

ITEM	SIZE / AMOUNT	# USED IN RECIPE	TOTAL	PRICE

DRYFOODS

MEATS

Equivalents: 1 lb. hamburger = 16 oz. = appx. 3 cups chunked
1 lb. boneless, skinless chicken = 16 oz. = appx. 2 1/2 cups chopped
1 boneless, skinless chicken breast = appx. 1 cup chopped
1 large onion = appx. 1 cup chopped

Shopping Planner

6 _____
7 _____
8 _____
9 _____
10 _____

CANNED FOODS

ITEM	SIZE / AMOUNT	# USED IN RECIPE	TOTAL	PRICE

FROZEN FOODS

ITEM	SIZE / AMOUNT	# USED IN RECIPE	TOTAL	PRICE

DAIRY SECTION

ITEM	SIZE / AMOUNT	# USED IN RECIPE	TOTAL	PRICE

Equivalents:

Total $

1 lb. cheese = appx. 4 cups grated
1 green pepper = appx. 1 cup chopped
2 medium carrots = appx. 1 cup shredded
2 stalks celery = appx. 1 cup chopped

Freezer Meals Index

Apricot Chicken

Serves 8   Serving Size 2/3 cup Chicken
                            2/3 cup Rice

Fat Grams 2   Calories 144

Ingredients

4 cups   chicken pieces *2D*

½ - 1 cup   nonfat Russian
                  dressing (to taste)

½ - 1 cup   Simply Fruit Apricot
                  Jam (to taste)

1 pkg.   onion soup mix***

Notes

Preparation Instructions

Combine and mix all ingredients. Bag and freeze.
When *thawed, heat in microwave for 5 - 7 minutes at 75% of maximum power.
Serve over brown rice.

* See section on **Thawing Instructions**
*** Possible MSG product. Read label.

Menu Suggestions

W ater 12 oz.
V eggie steamed peas,
            garden salad
G rain w.w. bread, brown rice
F ruit fruit cocktail on
P rotein nonfat cottage cheese
APRICOT CHICKEN

BBQ Beef

Serves 12   Serving Size 1/2 cup
Fat Grams 7   Calories 207

Ingredients

3 lb.	beef roast (beef brisket trimmed of all of the fat is best)
1 btl.	Hunt's BBQ sauce** (18 oz.)

Serving Suggestion

Serve:

• alone

• in a whole wheat hamburger bun.

• over a baked potato.

• over whole wheat pasta

• over brown rice.

Menu Suggestions

Water   12 oz.
Veggie   fresh steamed peas
Grain   baked potato
Fruit   fresh mixed fruit, cut-up
Protein   **BBQ BEEF**

Preparation Instructions

Cook the brisket in a slow oven (275 degrees) for 5 - 6 hours or in a crock pot over night. The beef is done when it tears apart in strings.

When the meat is done, drain the fat and pull the meat apart into strings. Mix together with the BBQ sauce. Pour into freezer bag and freeze.

When *thawed, heat through in microwave or on stove-top. If you heat it on the stove-top, use low heat and stir often.

* See section on **Thawing Instructions**
** See BBQ Sauce recipe in **Recipe Basics** section.

BBQ Chicken

Serves 6
Fat Grams 3

Serving Size 1 Cup
Calories 200

Ingredients

3 cups	chicken pieces
1 cup	onion
2 Tbl.	vinegar
2 Tbl.	brown sugar
¼ cup	lemon juice
3 Tbl.	Worcestershire sauce
1 cup	catsup
½ Tbl.	mustard, yellow prepared
1 cup	water
½ cup	chopped celery
to taste	salt and pepper

Preparation Instructions

Combine all ingredients and pour into freezer bag. Freeze.

When *thawed, bake uncovered at 350° for 45 minutes.

Serve over brown rice or whole wheat pasta.

* See section on **Thawing Instructions**

Menu Suggestions

Water 12 oz.
Veggie corn on the cob, green salad
Grain applesauce muffins
Fruit applesauce
Protein **BBQ CHICKEN**

California Citrus Chicken

Serves 6
Fat Grams 5

Serving Size 1 Breast or 1 cup
Calories 324

Ingredients

Sauce

¼ cup	apple cider vinegar
½ cup	orange juice frozen concentrate
1 cup	water
½ tsp.	dry yellow mustard
¼ tsp	tarragon seasoning
½ tsp	salt
2 Tbl.	honey or fructose
2 Tbl.	ULTRA GEL. or
1½ Tbl.	cornstarch
1 Tbl.	orange rind (optional)

Other

6 whole	chicken breasts or
6 cups	chicken pieces
1 cups	green pepper, diced
1/4 cup	red pepper, diced
4 Tbl.	green onion, chopped
1 cup	orange or mandarin orange sections (optional)
to taste	parsley

Preparation Instructions

Stir sauce ingredients together. Stir orange sections, chicken chunks or whole breasts and veggies into the sauce. Bag and freeze.

When *thawed, place in baking dish, cover and cook for 30 minutes at 350° .

To serve, remove from oven and garnish with parsley and grated orange rind. If chicken has been broken into pieces, serve over brown rice.

Menu Suggestions

Water	12 oz.
Veggie	steamed carrots
Grain	w.w. bread, brown rice
Fruit	fruit cocktail and nonfat cottage cheese
Protein	**CALIFORNIA CITRUS CHICKEN**

* See section on **Thawing Instructions**

Chicken & Rice Dinner

Serves 8
Fat Grams 4

Serving Size 1¼ Cup
Calories 252

Ingredients

4 cups	chicken pieces
2 cans	Cream of Chicken soup**
1 can	Cream of Celery soup**
½ - 1 pkg.	onion soup mix*** (to taste)
2 cups	water
1½ cups	long grain rice, uncooked (Instant)

Notes

Preparation Instructions

Combine all ingredients, put into freezer bag and freeze.

When *thawed, cover and bake at 375° for 50 minutes.

* See section on **Thawing Instructions**
** Campbell's Healthy Request soup - 10 1/2 oz or see recipe in Recipe Basics section.
*** Possible MSG product. Read label.

Menu Suggestions

Water	12 oz.
Veggie	Waldorf salad
Grain	whole grain roll
Fruit	peaches
Protein	**CHICKEN RICE DINNER**

Chicken Casserole

Serves 8
Fat Grams 9

Serving Size 2" x 4" Portion
Calories 306

Ingredients

2 cups	chicken pieces
1 cup	celery, chopped
½ cup	almonds, sliced
½ cup	water chestnuts, sliced, rinsed and drained
½ cup	green onions, chopped
1½ cup	chicken broth***
1 can	Cream of Mushroom soup**
3 cups	whole wheat elbow noodles cooked
	or
3 cups	brown rice, cooked
to taste	salt and pepper

Top With

4 Tbl.	sharp cheddar cheese

Preparation Instructions

Combine all ingredients in bag and freeze.

When *thawed, place in a 9" x 13" baking dish and bake covered for 20 minutes at 350°. Uncover, top with cheese and bake an additional 15 minutes.

Menu Suggestions

W_{ater}	12 oz.
V_{eggie}	garden salad, steamed zucchini
G_{rain}	brown rice
F_{ruit}	fruit salad
P_{rotein}	**CHICKEN CASSEROLE**

* See section on **Thawing Instructions**
** Campbell's Healthy Request soup -10 1/2 oz or see recipe in Recipe Basics section.
*** Possible MSG product. Read label.

For Thicker Sauce:

to taste	add cornstarch or ULTRA GEL®

Chicken Chow Mein

Serves 8   Serving Size 1 1/3 Cup
Fat Grams 3   Calories 154

Ingredients

Sauce

2 cups	chicken broth***
3 cups	chicken pieces
½ cup	onion
1 cup	celery, sliced
2 cup	carrots, sliced
1 cup	green pepper (chop)
8 oz.	fresh mushrooms (sliced)
	soy sauce (to taste)
1 Tbl.	Butter Buds liquid (or to taste)
4 Tbl.	whole wheat flour
	sprouts (optional at time of serving)
	brown rice (optional at time of serving)

* See section on **Thawing Instructions**
*** Possible MSG product. Read label.

Preparation Instructions

Brown onion, celery, carrots, green pepper and mushrooms in Butter Buds until tender, but still somewhat crispy. Sprinkle about four tablespoons flour on top of vegetables. Pour chicken broth over and stir until bubbly. Season with soy sauce to desired taste. Add chicken. Pour into bag and freeze.

When *thawed, heat through in microwave at 75% power and serve over brown rice or sprouts.

Menu Suggestions

W$_{ater}$	12 oz.
V$_{eggie}$	steamed peas and carrots
G$_{rain}$	brown rice
F$_{ruit}$	fruit cocktail
P$_{rotein}$	**CHICKEN CHOW MEIN**

Chicken Cordon Blue

Serves 6   Serving Size 1 Breast
Fat Grams 9   Calories 371

Ingredients

6	chicken breasts, WHOLE, COOKED
6 slices	Louis Rich turkey ham (thinly sliced)
6 oz.	part skim mozzarella cheese (thinly sliced)

Topping

2 cans	Cream of Chicken Soup**
8 oz.	nonfat sour cream

Preparation Instructions

Set aside 6 whole chicken breasts after cooking. Layer each chicken breast with sliced turkey-ham and sliced cheese. Put toothpicks in at an angle to secure the layers. Put into freezer bag. Mix soup and sour cream. Pour over chicken in bag. Freeze.

When *thawed, heat through in microwave at 75% maximum power.

Serve over a bed of brown rice.

* See section on **Thawing Instructions**
** Campbell's Healthy Request soup -10 1/2 oz or see recipe in Recipe Basics section.

Menu Suggestions

Water 12 oz.
Veggie baked squash, garden salad
Grain w.w. bread, brown rice
Fruit fruit in season
Protein **CORDON BLUE**

\\

Chicken Cordon Blue Casserole

Serves 8   Serving Size 1 Cup Sauce, 1 Cup Rice
Fat Grams 9   Calories 526

Ingredients

4 cups	chicken pieces
2 cans	Cream of Chicken soup**
8 oz.	nonfat sour cream
2 cups	Louis Rich Turkey-ham, diced
8 oz.	Frigo Truly Lite Ricotta Cheese, nonfat
1 cup	whole wheat bread crumbs
8 cups	brown rice, pre-cooked (freeze seperately; thaw and use at time of serving.)

Preparation Instructions

Using the Chicken Cordon Blue recipe from previous page, you can make a casserole.

Mix togethr all ingredients, label and freeze.

When *thawed, place in a baking dish and bake casserole uncovered at 350° for 40 minutes (until bubbly).

Top with some bread crumbs (optional), bake additional five minutes and serve over rice.

* See section on **Thawing Instructions**
** Campbell's Healthy Request soup -10 1/2 oz
   or see recipe in Recipe Basics section.

Menu Suggestions

W$_{ater}$ 12 oz.
V$_{eggie}$ steamed broccoli and coliflower
G$_{rain}$ bed of brown rice
F$_{ruit}$ fruit in season
P$_{rotein}$ **CCB CASSEROLE**

Chicken Divan

Serves 6
Fat Grams 3

Serving Size 1/6 Portion
Calories 250

Ingredients

16 oz.	broccoli fresh or frozen, chopped
3 cups	chicken pieces
1 can	Cream of Chicken soup**
½ cup	cheddar cheese, grated
½ cup	nonfat plain yogurt
1 tsp.	lemon juice
¼ tsp.	curry
1 can	mushrooms (4 oz.)(drained)
1 cup	onion, chopped

Toppings

1 cup	bread cubes, dried
1 Tbl.	parsley flakes
6 cups	brown rice, cooked

Preparation Instructions

Combine all ingredients and pour into bag and freeze.

When *thawed, sprinkle top with bread cubes and parsley and bake in baking dish uncovered at 350° for 50 minutes.

Serve on a bed of brown rice or serve by itself.

* See section on **Thawing Instructions**
** Campbell's Healthy Request soup - 10 1/2 oz or see recipe in Recipe Basics section.

Menu Suggestions

Water	12 oz.
Veggie	tossed salad
Grain	w.w. rolls, brown rice
Fruit	peach
Protein	**CHICKEN DIVAN**

Chicken Enchiladas

Serves 12
Fat Grams 5

Serving Size = 1 Enchilada
Calories 293

Ingredients

Filling

¼ tsp.	cumin
½ tsp.	chili powder
¼ tsp.	pepper
¼ tsp.	salt
½ Tbl.	lemon juice
¼ tsp.	garlic powder
3 cups	chicken pieces, broken
1 cup	white onion, diced
¾ cup	red pepper, diced
¾ cup	green pepper, diced
½ cup	fat free sour cream
½ cup	nonfat cottage cheese
1 cup	skim mozzarella cheese

Other

1 pkg.	w.w. flour tortillas (1 fat gram each)

Topping Mild to Spicy

10 oz.	tomato sauce **or**
1/3 cup	picante sauce **or**
10 oz.	enchilada sauce
1/3 cup	skim mozzarella cheese

* See section on
**Thawing
Instructions**

Preparation Instructions

Combine filling ingredients in a bowl. Spoon a line (two heaping tablespoons) of mixture through the center of a tortilla. Fold in tortilla sides and roll up the tortilla from the bottom. Place tortillas snuggly against each other inside a gallon-size freezer bag. Label, seal and place in freezer.

When *thawed, pour a layer of your favorite topping sauce on the bottom of a 9" x 13" pan. Place enchiladas side by side and pour the remainder of the sauce over the top. Sprinkle with a little bit of cheese, cover and bake at 350° for 30 minutes.

Serve over a bed of shredded lettuce and chopped tomatoes.

Menu Suggestions

W_ater	12 oz.
V_eggie	included in meal
G_rain	included in tortilla
F_ruit	tomatoes
P_rotein	**Chicken Enchiladas**

Chicken Fajitas

Serves 10   Serving Size 1 Tortilla
Fat Grams 6   Calories 294

Ingredients

Mixture

3 cups   chicken pieces

1 btl.   picante sauce
         (16 oz.)

Topping

1 Tbl.   part skim mozzerella
         cheese per fajita

To Serve

1 pkg.   whole wheat flour
         tortillas

Menu Suggestions

W_{ater} 12 oz.
V_{eggie} refried beans with
             part skim
             mozzarella cheese
             sprinkled, melted on
             top
G_{rain} included in tortilla
F_{ruit} 1/2 sliced avacado
P_{rotein} **CHICKEN FAJITA**

Preparation Instructions

Combine mixture and freeze mixture in bag.

When *thawed, spread ¼ cup mixture on flour tortilla. Sprinkle mozzarella cheese lightly on top. Microwave each tortilla flat for 45 seconds on high. Roll up and serve.

Single Servings

This recipe works well for single serving portions. Spread a single tortilla with mixture, roll up, place in freezer bag and freeze.

To serve, place on plate and microwave on high for two minutes. Top with hot sauce.

* See section on **Thawing Instructions**

Chicken Lasagna

51

Serves 18 Serving Size 2 5/8"x 2 5/8"
Fat Grams 8 Calories 224

Ingredients

Filling

1 cup	onions, chopped
1 cup	green pepper, chopped
2 cans	Cream of Chicken soup**
1/3 cup	skim milk
1 cup	mushrooms, fresh sliced
1 Tbl.	pimiento, diced
1 tsp.	basil, dried, crushed
3 cups	nonfat cottage cheese (24 oz.)
1 ½ cups	Frigo Truly Lite skim mozzarella, shredded
¼ cup	Parmesan cheese, grated (or for more flavor use ½ cup and add 1 FG per serving)
4 cups	chicken, chopped, cooked

Other

8 oz.	whole wheat lasagna noodles
½ cup	cheddar cheese, shredded

Menu Suggestions

Water	12 oz.
Veggie	tossed green salad
Grain	w.w. garlic toast
Fruit	nectarine slices
Protein	**LASAGNA**

Preparation Instructions

This recipe makes two 8" x 8" pans of lasagna. If your family is small you will use only one at a time. If your family is large, cook both pans.

Mix filling ingredients together in a large bowl. Line pans with tin foil and spread 1 cup of filling on bottom of each pan. Cook noodles for three minutes (boiling), break noodles to fit the pans and layer over filling. Repeat whole process. Evenly divide remaining filling for the final layer. Sprinkle with paprika. Freeze over night.

Next day, remove from pan and carefully peel foil away. Label freezer bag, place lasagna inside, remove air and return to freezer.

To prepare, spray original pan with cooking spray and put lasagna in pan. Sprinkle cheddar cheese on top. Bake from frozen to done for one hour at 400° covered.

To serve, add salt and pepper to taste.

* See section on **Thawing Instructions**
** Campbell's Healthy Request soup -10 1/2 oz or See Recipe Basics section.

5

Chicken Noodle Soup

52

Serves 8
Fat Grams 3

Serving Size 1 1/2 Cup
Calories 260

Ingredients

6 cups or more	chicken broth Homemade Chicken Broth Recipe**** **or** canned broth***
2 cups	chicken pieces
1½ cup	carrots, chopped
1½ cup	celery
1 cup	onion
11 oz.	frozen homemade whole wheat noodles
to taste	salt and pepper

Menu Suggestions

W$_{ater}$	12 oz.
V$_{eggie}$	fresh vegetable salad
G$_{rain}$	w.w. toast
F$_{ruit}$	sliced green apples
P$_{rotein}$	**CHICKEN NOODLE SOUP**

Preparation Instructions

Bring chicken broth to a boil. Add carrots, celery and onions. (Use your leftover vegetables.) Add homemade w.w. noodles and boil until noodles are tender. Add at least two cups chicken pieces. Bag and freeze.

When *thawed, simmer for 30 minutes until heated through and enjoy!

****Homemade Chicken Broth

Strain broth that you cooked your chicken in. Skim off the foam. Put in a clean pan and chill overnight. The next morning, remove congealed fat from top of broth. Add enough water to make as much soup as you want. Salt and pepper to taste. Bring this to a boil. Add in other ingredients as noted above.

* See section on **Thawing Instructions**
*** Possible MSG product. Read label.
**** See Homemade Chicken Broth recipe above.

Chicken Pockets

Serves 12   Serving Size 2 Pockets
Fat Grams 4   Calories 356

Ingredients

Filling

8 oz.	nonfat cream cheese
¼ cup	green onions, chopped
3 cups	chicken pieces

Other

1 pkg.	Rhodes Lite frozen whole wheat dinner rolls
½ cup	whole wheat bread crumbs

Topping

1 can	Cream of chicken soup**

* See section on **Thawing Instructions**
** Campbell's Healthy Request soup - 10 1/2 oz
   or see recipe in Recipe Basics section.

Preparation Instructions

Combine filling ingredients. Stretch the roll and wrap it around a spoonful of chicken mixture. Seal edges tightly. Pat bread crumbs on top. Put into bag and freeze.

When *thawed, bake uncovered at 350° for 30 minutes (until golden brown). Heat cream of chicken soup with enough milk for desired consistency to make gravy and pour over each roll. Enjoy with a vegetable and salad.

Menu Suggestions

Water	12 oz.
Veggie	steamed broccoli, cauliflower and carrots
Grain	included in pocket
Fruit	fruit cup
Protein	**CHICKEN POCKET**

Chicken Spaghetti

Serves 6　　　　　Serving Size 1/6 Portion
Fat Grams 7　　　Calories 323

Ingredients

3 cups	chicken pieces
1 cup	chicken broth**
1 pkg.	whole wheat spaghetti noodles (8 oz.)
1 cup	onion
1 can	tomatoes, drained (14 oz.)
1 can	mushrooms, drained (4 oz.)
	or
½ cup	mushrooms, fresh sliced
¼ cup	black olives, chopped
1 tsp.	Worcestershire sauce
¼ tsp.	garlic salt
¼ cup	Parmesan cheese, fresh
to taste	salt and pepper

* See section on **Thawing Instructions**
** Campbell's Healthy Request soup - 10 1/2 oz
　 or see recipe in Recipe Basics section

Preparation Instructions

Cook noodles as instructed on package until almost done (approximately three minutes in boiling water). Combine all ingredients and put in freezer bag.

When *thawed, cover and bake for 50 minutes at 375°.

Notes

Menu Suggestions

W_{ater}　12 oz.
V_{eggie}　garden salad, fat free Italian dressing
G_{rain}　garlic bread
F_{ruit}　sliced tomatoes
P_{rotein}　**CHICKEN SPAGHETTI**

Chicken Stir Fry

55

Serves 6   Serving Size 3/4 cups Stir Fry, 1 cup Rice
Fat Grams 3   Calories 222

Ingredients

Chicken Marinate

3 cups	chicken pieces
¼ cup	soy sauce, low sodium
½ cup	apple juice concentrate, frozen
¼ tsp.	ginger
1 Tbl.	honey
¼ cup	orange juice concentrate, frozen
3 Tbl.	ULTRA GEL®^
	or
2 Tbl.	Cornstarch
1 cup	water

Vegetables

1 pkg.	Chinese vegetables, frozen
	or

Freshly Chopped

broccoli, onions, green and/or red pepper, celery, bamboo shoots, carrots and water chestnuts

Serve With

6 cups	brown rice

* See section on **Thawing Instructions**
^ See Product Section

Preparation Instructions

Combine chicken marinate ingredients and pour into a bag. Seal and freeze.

When *thawed, stir chicken marinate in a Wok at 350° or fry pan on medium-high until chicken is hot. Stir in frozen vegetables, cover and simmer for five minutes until hot, but crisp. If using fresh vegetables (fresh is preferred), stir until vegetables are warm, but still crisp, approximately two to three minutes.

Serve over rice. Add additional soy sauce to rice for richer flavor.

Option

Add 1 oz. unsalted peanuts (2.5 fat grams per serving added)
Add 1 oz. lightly salted cashews (2.5 fat grams per serving added)

Menu Suggestions

W_{ater}	12 oz.
V_{eggie}	baked sweet potato
	garden salad
G_{rain}	brown rice
F_{ruit}	fresh strawberries
P_{rotein}	**CHICKEN STIR FRY**

Chili

Serves 10   Serving Size 1½ cup
Fat Grams 7   Calories 427

Ingredients

Sauce

1½ cups ground beef, extra lean

1 cup   bulgur wheat****

1 cup   onion

1 qt.   stewed tomatoes

1 can   tomato sauce (8 oz.)

1 cup   salsa

1 can   kidney beans with juice

1 can   pinto beans with juice

1 can   red beans with juice

1 can   great Northern white beans with juice

1 can   garbonzo beans with juice

1 can   blackeyed peas with juice

1 - 2 Tbl. chili powder

¼-½ cup ULTRA GEL.

or

¼ cup   cornstarch
(optional for thicker chili)

Preparation Instructions

Combine all ingredients and freeze.

When *thawed, simmer over low heat for 35 - 40 minutes.

Notes

Menu Suggestions

W_{ater} 12 oz.
V_{eggie} included in chili
G_{rain} w.w. bread sticks
F_{ruit} fruit salad
P_{rotein} **CHILI**

* See section on **Thawing Instructions**
**** See Bulgar Wheat recipe in Recipe Basics section

Chinese Sundaes

Serves 6   Serving Size 1 Cup
Fat Grams 4   Calories 171

Ingredients

3 cups	chicken pieces
2 cups	chicken broth***
4½ Tbl.	ULTRA GEL®^
	or
4 Tbl.	cornstarch
	mixed with
4 Tbl.	cold water
1 cup	carrots, sliced
½ tsp.	basil
¼ tsp.	pepper
½ tsp.	salt
1 can	Cream of Chicken soup**

Serving

optional	chow mein noodles
optional	brown rice

* See section on **Thawing Instructions**
** Campbell's Healthy Request soup - 10 1/2 oz
    or see recipe in Recipe Basics section.
*** Possible MSG product. Read label.
^   See Product Section for description.

Preparation Instructions

Combine all ingredients except chicken pieces and Chow Mein noodles. Bring to a boil to thicken. Add chicken, pour into bag and freeze.

When *thawed, heat in the microwave for about three minutes at 75% power. Serve over rice or chow mein noodles (high fat item...be conservative).

Stack with a variety of your favorite toppings. Topping suggestions: chopped tomatoes, chopped green pepper, coconut, sliced celery, pineapple tidbits, grated cheese, chopped green onion, or anything else that sounds good to you!

Menu Suggestions

Water	12 oz.
Veggie	included in sundaes
Grain	brown rice
Fruit	pineapple
Protein	**CHINESE SUNDAES**

Fish and Herb Broil

Serves 8   Serving Size 1/8 Portion
Fat Grams 2   Calories 144

Ingredients

2 lbs.	fresh fish of your choice (halibut, cod, haddock, orange roughy, etc.)

Sauce

2 pkts.	Butter Buds
1¼ tsp.	salt
to taste	pepper
½ tsp.	dried basil, crushed
1¼ cup	tomatoes, chopped
2 cups	mushrooms, fresh, sliced
4 Tbl.	green onions, chopped
optional	lemon wedges

Menu Suggestions

Water	12 oz.
Veggie	baked Hubbard squash, salad
Grain	w.w. muffins
Fruit	sliced peaches
Protein	**FISH & HERB BROIL**

Broiling Instructions

Remove fish from sauce and broil for three to four minutes in baking dish. Turn fish over, pour sauce on top and broil for an additional five to seven minutes or until flaky through the thick part of the fish.

Alternative Preparation Instruction

Combine all ingredients (including fish) in a freezer bag, seal and freeze.

When *thawed, allow 10 minutes cooking time for each inch of thickness in fillets. Bake at 450° in a covered baking dish.

To serve, sprinkle a small amount of basil over the top and garnish with lemon wedges and parsley.

See Tartar Sauce recipe in Recipe Basics section.

* See section on **Thawing Instructions**

Halibut

Serves 8
Fat Grams 3

Serving Size 1/8 Portion
Calories 145

Ingredients

2 lbs.	halibut fish fillets, fresh
1 pkg.	Butter Buds®
1	onion, finely chopped
to taste	parsley, fresh, chopped
4 Tbl.	lemon juice, fresh
optional	lemon wedges
to taste	salt and pepper

Preparation Instructions

Combine all ingredients (raw), bag, seal and freeze.
When *thawed, allow 10 minutes cooking time for each inch of thickness in fillets. Bake at 450° in a covered baking dish.
Serve immediately with lemon wedges and/or tartar sauce, sprinkled with fresh, chopped parsley.

* See section on **Thawing Instructions**
** See Recipe Basics Section

Menu Suggestions

W_{ater}	12 oz.
V_{eggie}	steamed veggies and Cheese Sauce**
G_{rain}	parsleyed new potatoes
F_{ruit}	sliced oranges
P_{rotein}	**HALIBUT**

Hamballs In Hawaiian Sauce

Serves 6
Fat Grams 7

Serving Size 7 Meatballs
Calories 413

Ingredients

Sauce

¼ cup	honey
¼ cup	black strap mollasses
½ tsp.	salt
¼ cup	ULTRA GEL .^
	or
3 Tbl.	cornstarch
2 cans	pineapple,crushed plus juice(13.5 oz.)

Meat

4 cups	Louis Rich Turkey-ham (ground by your butcher)
1 cup	whole wheat bread crumbs (see recipe in this book)
1	egg, beaten

Preparation Instructions

Combine turkey-ham, bread crumbs, and egg. Make into ½ inch balls. Bake for 30 minutes at 350°.

While baking, mix sauce and cook over medium heat to thicken. Add crushed pineapple and heat through. Put ham balls into freezer bag. Pour slightly cooled sauce into bag over baked ham balls. Freeze.

When *thawed , place in a covered casserole dish or cover with plastic wrap. Cook for three minutes at 75% power in microwave. Stir and continue cooking for three more minutes.

Serve over rice.

* See section on **Thawing Instructions.**
^ See **Product section** for description.

Menu Suggestions

W$_{ater}$	12 oz.
V$_{eggie}$	steamed broccoli
G$_{rain}$	brown rice
F$_{ruit}$	pineapple
P$_{rotein}$	**HAMBALLS IN HAWAIIAN SAUCE**

2

Ham Dinner

1 Slice
Fat Grams 2

Serving Size 2 oz.
Calories 70

61

Ingredients

turkey-ham roast

optional pineapple chunks
plus juice

optional cloves

Notes

* See section on **Thawing Instructions**

Preparation Instructions

Have your butcher cut enough turkey-ham slices bologna thick for your family (with a few extra for hungry people!) Simply freeze these in a smaller freezer bag.

When you want a fast "Sunday" meal, pull out the ham slices, heat them through in the microwave and serve with baked potatoes, vegetable, and salad.

Cooking Options

1. Pan fry the turkey-ham in pinapple chunks and juice.
2. Sprinkle ham with cloves for a spicy flavor.

Menu Suggestions

W_{ater}   12 oz.
V_{eggie}   steamed broccoli, fresh green salad
G_{rain}   baked potato
F_{ruit}   pineapple slices
P_{rotein}   **HAM DINNER**

62

Ham Fried Rice

Serves 6
Fat Grams 4

Serving Size 1 Cup
Calories 228

Ingredients

1½ cups turkey-ham,diced

1 can   water chestnuts,
         sliced, drained
         (8oz.)

1 can   mushrooms, drained
         (4 oz.)

¼ cup   green pepper,
         chopped

1 cup   petite peas, frozen

3 cup   brown rice, cooked

1 whole egg **plus**

2   egg whites
         (scramble all)

2 Tbl.   soy sauce

Preparation Instructions

Combine all ingredients.
Pour into freezer bag.
When *thawed, stir fry in
about one tablespoon olive,
peanut or Canola oil until
heated through.

* See section on **Thawing Instructions**

Menu Suggestions

Water   12 oz.
Veggie   frozen sweet pea
             pods
Grain   w.w. roll
Fruit   frozen banana slices
Protein **HAM FRIED RICE**

Ham Rolls

Serves 12   Serving Size 2 Rolls
Fat Grams 4   Calories 342

Ingredients

Filling

1 pkg.	whole wheat dinner rolls, frozen (Rhodes -Texas rolls)
1½ cups	ricotta cheese
2 cups	turkey-ham, chopped
½ cup	onion, chopped
½ cup	mushroom pieces, (or 1, 4 oz. can)

Sauce

1 can	Cream of Mushroom soup**
½ cup	skim milk

Option

Use garlic & onion spaghetti sauce in place of soup and milk

* See section on **Thawing Instructions**
** Campbell's Healthy Request soup -10 1/2 oz or see recipe in Recipe Basics section.

Preparation Instructions

Soften dough in microwave on defrost for several minutes. Combine filling ingredients. Stretch out one roll (dough) and spoon filling inside, then pulling up the outer edges of the roll, seal edges well. Continue with this procedure until filling and/or rolls are gone. Put into bag and freeze. The morning you plan to cook this dish, remove from freezer and place in refrigerator to thaw.

When *thawed, place on a cookie sheet, spray tops with butter flavored cooking spray and bake uncovered at 375° for 45 minutes.

Heat soup with skim milk to make a gravy to pour over the top.

Menu Suggestions

W_{ater}	12 oz.
V_{eggie}	steamed mixed vegetables
G_{rain}	included in rolls
F_{ruit}	fruit cocktail on nonfat cottage cheese
P_{rotein}	**HAM ROLLS**

Hawaiian Chicken

Serves 6
Fat Grams 4

Serving Size 1 Cup
Calories 222

Ingredients

1 cup	onion, chopped
1	green pepper cut in strips
2 cans	Cream of Chicken soup**
1 can	pineapple tidbits with juice (15 oz.)
2 cups	chicken pieces
2 tsp.	soy sauce

When Serving

optional tomatoes

4-6 cups brown rice

Preparation Instructions

Combine all ingredients, bag and freeze.

When *thawed, heat thoroughly in saucepan over low heat (stirring often) and serve over rice. If you opt for the tomatoes, just cut them up and put them on top. It's delicious!

Notes

Menu Suggestions

W_{ater}	12 oz.
V_{eggie}	oven baked fries
G_{rain}	whole grain roll
F_{ruit}	sliced oranges
P_{rotein}	**HAWAIIAN CHICKEN**

* See section on **Thawing Instructions**
** Campbell's Healthy Request soup - 10 1/2 oz or see recipe in Recipe Basics section.

Italian Chicken Casserole

Serves 6
Fat Grams 6

Serving Size 1 Cup
Calories 288

Ingredients

3 cups	chicken breast, RAW cut-up
½ cup	nonfat Italian dressing
1½ cup	whole wheat bread crumbs^
1 cup	mushrooms, fresh, sliced
1 cup	Frigo Truly Lite part skim mozzarella cheese
1 cup	nonfat cottage cheese
½ cup	chicken broth***

Preparation Instructions

Place bread crumbs in a zip-lock bag. Coat chicken in Italian dressing and put in bag. Shake bag gently to coat chicken with crumbs. Brown chicken in one tablespoon virgin olive oil or Canola oil in a frying pan. Put on bottom of freezer bag. Top with sliced mushrooms and cheese. Combine cottage cheese and chicken broth. Pour over top. Freeze.

When *thawed, bake uncovered at 350° for 35 minutes.

* See section on **Thawing Instructions**
*** Possible MSG product. Read label.
^ See recipe in Recipe Basics section.

Menu Suggestions

Water	12 oz.
Veggie	steamed zucchini, fresh garden salad
Grain	w.w. rolls
Fruit	fruit salad
Protein	**ITALIAN CHICKEN CASSEROLE**

Lasagna

Serves 12
Fat Grams 13

Serving Size 2 5/8" x 4" Piece
Calories 340

Ingredients

1½ cup	ground beef, extra lean
3/4 cup	bulgur wheat**** cracked, cooked
¼ tsp.	garlic powder
½ cup	onion, diced
8 oz.	tomato sauce
1 crtn.	nonfat cottage cheese (2 lb.)
1 btl.	Campbell's Spaghetti Sauce (26½ oz.)
1 cup	sharp cheddar cheese
16 oz.	ricotta cheese, nonfat
1/3 cup	Parmesan cheese
1 pkg.	whole wheat lasagna noodles (dry) (8 oz.)

Menu Suggestions

Water	12 oz.
Veggie	fresh steamed peas and onion, salad
Grain	garlic w.w. bread
Fruit	fruit in season
Protein	**LASAGNA**

* See section on **Thawing Instructions**
**** See **Bulgur Wheat** recipe in **Recipe Basics**

Preparation Instructions

This recipe makes one 9" x 13" pan of lasagna, but if you freeze it in the pan, you will have to buy extra large (2 gallon) freezer bags. It's easier to build the lasagna in two 8" x 8" baking dishes. If your family is small (4-5) you will use only one at a time. If your family is large, cook both pans.

Mix spaghetti sauce with wheat, tomato sauce, ground beef, onion and garlic. Line pans with tin foil and spread ¼ sauce mixture on bottom of each pan. Break noodles to fit the pans and layer over sauce. Spread ½ cup cottage cheese, followed by ¼ cup cheddar and ½ cup ricotta cheese. Repeat whole process. Sprinkle with Parmesan cheese. Freeze over night.

Next day, remove from pan and carefully peel foil away. Place in freezer bag, remove air and return to freezer.

To serve, bake from frozen to done. Spray original pan with cooking spray and put lasagna in pan. Bake 1 hour and 30 minutes at 400° covered.

Meatballs

Serves 10   Serving Size 7 Meatballs + Sauce

Fat Grams 10   Calories 332

Ingredients

Meat

2 cups	ground beef, extra lean, fresh, *RAW*
1 cup	bulgur wheat, **** cracked and boiled
1 tsp.	salt (or to taste)
½ tsp.	pepper (or to taste)
¼ cup	onion, chopped
4 slices	w.w. bread, cubed
2	eggs
2	egg whites
½ cup	skim milk

Sauce

1 can	Cream of Chicken soup**
½ cup	onion, chopped
8 oz.	nonfat cottage cheese
1 can	Cream of Mushroom soup**
1 cup	skim milk
to taste	salt and pepper

Preparation Instructions

Crack and boil bulgar wheat for 5 minutes or until tender (doubling the amount.)

Combine all ingredients for meatballs and form approximately 70, 1/2" meatballs. Place on cookie sheet and brown in 400° oven for about 20 minutes. Drain any grease. Mix ingredients for sauce and combine with meatballs. Bag and freeze.

When *thawed, place in a covered casserole dish and bake at 350° for one hour.

Serve over rice or noodles.

Menu Suggestions

W_{ater}	12 oz.
V_{eggie}	steamed green beans, salad
G_{rain}	rice or ww. noodles
F_{ruit}	fruit in season
P_{rotein}	**MEATBALLS**

* See section on **Thawing Instructions**

** Campbell's Healthy Request soup -10 1/2 oz or see recipe in Recipe Basics section.

**** See Bulgur Wheat recipe in Recipe Basics section.

Meatless Enchiladas

Serves 14   Serving Size = 1 Enchilada
Fat Grams 4   Calories 259

Ingredients

Filling

1 Tbl.	chili powder
½ tsp.	ground cumin
¼ tsp.	garlic powder
½ cup	picante sauce
½ cup	green onions, diced or white onions pureed
½ cup	green peppers, diced
½ cup	part skim mozzarella cheese
½ cup	nonfat cottage cheese, drained
½ cup	nonfat sour cream
1 can	vegetarian refried beans (16 oz.)

Other

1 pkg.	whole wheat flour tortillas (1.5 FG)

Sauce

Mix:

8 oz.	enchilada sauce
½ cup	picante sauce

Sprinkle:

½ cup	skim mozzarella cheese

Fresh Toppings Prior to Serving:

1 cup	lettuce, shredded per enchilada

Preparation Instructions

Combine ingredients for filling in a mixing bowl. Spread two tablespoons of filling across the center of the tortilla. Fold in the sides of the tortilla about 1" and roll the tortilla up from the bottom. Place inside a gallon size freezer bag, side by side. Seal and freeze.

To serve, remove frozen enchiladas from bag and place in 9" x 13" pan. Pour sauce over the top and sprinkle with mozzarella cheese. Cover with foil and bake at 350° for 45 minutes from frozen to done.

Individual Servings

Place two enchiladas in a small freezer bag. To serve, place frozen enchiladas on a plate, cover with sauce, sprinkle with cheese and microwave four to five minutes on high.

Menu Suggestions

Water	12 oz.
Veggie	included in enchilada
Grain	included in tortilla
Fruit	sliced tomatoes
Protein	**Picante Enchiladas**

Mexican Chicken

Serves 8
Fat Grams 8

Serving Size 1 Cup
Calories 250

Ingredients

Mixture

4 cups	chicken pieces
½ cup	cheddar cheese
½ cup	skim mozzarella cheese (Frigo Truly Lite)
1 can	Green chilies, chopped (4 oz.)
½ cup	nonfat cottage cheese
1 cup	onion, chopped
¼ tsp.	chili powder
¼ tsp.	oregano
1 cup	chicken broth ***

Other

1 doz.	soft corn tortillas (for method 1)
	or
1 doz.	Janet Lee's Crisp Corn Tortillas (for method 2)

* See section on **Thawing Instructions**
*** Possible MSG product. Read label.

Preparation Instructions

Combine all ingredients except tortillas.

METHOD 1:

In freezer bag, layer four flat tortillas (spread out as much as possible). On top of this, spread all of the mixture.
When *thawed, bake covered at 375° for 30 minutes, then uncover and bake additional 15 to 20 minutes.

METHOD 2:

Put mixture in freezer bag, seal and freeze.
When *thawed, cook covered for 40 minutes at 375°. Serve over one crumbled taco shell.

Menu Suggestions

Water	12 oz.
Veggie	**fresh veggie salad**
Grain	**included in tortilla**
Fruit	chopped tomatoes
Protein	**MEXICAN CHICKEN**

4

70

Party Time Turkey

Serves 6
Fat Grams 3

Serving Size 1, 4 oz. breast
Calories 195

Ingredients

6 pieces	turkey breasts, boneless, skinless (appx. 4 oz. each)
½ cup	onion, chopped
1½ cup	celery, chopped
2 Tbl.	pimentos
¼ cup	green pepper
2 tsp.	lemon juice
½ cup	skim milk
½ can	Cream of Chicken soup**
1 cup	plain yogurt
½ tsp.	tarragon seasoning (optional)

Preparation Instructions

Prepare 4 oz. portion of turkey breast or 1 chicken breast for each person in your family. Mix other ingredients together. Label one gallon freezer bag. Place meat in bag side-by-side, pour sauce on top, seal and freeze.

After *thawed, place in a baking dish, cover and bake in oven for 45 minutes at 350°.

* See section on **Thawing Instructions**
** Campbell's Healthy Request soup -10 1/2 oz or see recipe in Recipe Basics section.

Menu Suggestions

W_ater 12 oz.
V_eggie fresh steamed green beans
G_rain whole wheat dressing
F_ruit peaches
P_rotein **PARTY TIME TURKEY**

Shepherd's Pie

Serves 8
Fat Grams: Beef Mix 13
           Chicken 5

Serving Size 4" x 4"
Calories: Beef Mix 332
         Chicken 261

Ingredients

Meat

3 cups	chicken, ground (grind in food processor)

Or Mix

2 cups	ground beef, extra lean **plus**
½ cup	dry bulgur wheat****

Combine With

1 cup	onion, diced
1½ cups	green beans, fresh snapped or frozen
1 can	Cream of Chicken Soup**
1 can	Cream of Mushroom Soup**
½ cup	skim milk
½ cup	cheddar cheese

Top With

1 pkg.	hashbrowns, frozen (grated or chunked)
to taste	salt (appx. ½ tsp.)
to taste	pepper (appx. ¼ tsp.)
to taste	paprika

Preparation Instructions

Crack 1/2 cup bulgar wheat in blender, boil in water for five minutes or until tender. Combine all ingredients, bag and freeze.

When *thawed, layer with hashbrown and bake uncovered at 350° for 40 minutes. Top with two tablespoon sharp cheddar cheese and Paprika.

• Add one fat gram per serving for additional cheese topping.

NOTE

Use one can Tomato soup** in place of Cream of Chicken soup** when using hamburger mix.

You can also replace both Cream soups with Tomato soup.

FOR A CHEWIER TEXTURE: Leave wheat in whole kernals.

Menu Suggestions

Water	12 oz.
Veggie	fresh veggie plate and dip
Grain	w.w. roll
Fruit	sliced apples
Protein	**HASHBROWN CASSEROLE**

* See section on **Thawing Instructions**
** Campbell's Healthy Request soup -10 1/2 oz or see recipe in Recipe Basics section.
**** See Bulgar Wheat in Recipe Basics Sec.

Sloppy Joes

Serves 12
Fat Grams 6

Serving Size 1 Sloppy Joe
Calories 247

Ingredients

½ cup	onion, pureed
	or
1 cup	onion, chopped
1 can	tomato sauce (8 oz.)
1 can	chicken gumbo soup***
¼ cup	catsup
1 tbl.	Worcestershire sauce
½ Tbl.	mustard
1½ cups	ground beef, extra lean
1 cup	bulgur wheat,**** cracked
¼ cup	green pepper, finely chopped
12	whole wheat hamburger buns

Menu Suggestions

W_{ater}   12 oz.
V_{eggie}   baked beans, tossed salad
G_{rain}   w.w. bun
F_{ruit}   orange slices
P_{rotein}   **SLOPPY JOES**

Preparation Instructions

Crack bulgur wheat in a blender or food processor. Add all ingredients together, mixing well. Freeze.

*Thaw, place in bowl and microwave on 75% maximum heat for about 10 minutes. Stir occasionally.

Serve in a whole grain bun.

Sweeter Recipe Variation

Fat Grams 6   Calories 251

1½ cup	ground beef, extra lean
1 cup	bulgur wheat
½ cup	onion
½ cup	green pepper
1 tsp.	salt
3/4 cup	ketchup
½ cup	water
1 Tbl.	honey
1 Tbl.	vinegar
1 Tbl.	Worcestershire sauce

Texture Variation

For a chewier sandwich, leave the bulgur wheat in it's full kernel.

* See section on **Thawing Instructions**
*** Possible MSG product. Read label.
**** See Bulgur Wheat recipe in Recipe Basics section

Slow Simmering Bean Soup

Serves 14   Serving Size 1 Cup
Fat Grams Trace   Calories 128

73

Ingredients

1 can	red kidney beans, (15 oz.) drained
1 can	pinto beans (15 oz.)
3 cups	water
1 can	Mexican style stewed tomatoes (14 oz.)
1 pkg.	corn (16 oz.), frozen
1 cup	carrots, sliced
1 cup	onion, chopped
1 can	green chilies, chopped (4 oz.)
2 Tbs.	beef bouillon granules***
1 tsp.	chili powder
¼ tsp.	minced garlic

* See section on **Thawing Instructions**
*** Possible MSG product. Read label.

Preparation Instructions

Combine all ingredients and simmer for two to three hours on the stove. Pour into freezer bag and place in freezer.

When *thawed, heat through in microwave or all day in a slow crock pot.

Notes

Menu Suggestions

W_ater	12 oz.
V_eggie	veggie salad
G_rain	w.w. bread sticks
F_ruit	sliced pears
P_rotein	**SLOW SIMMERING BEAN SOUP**

Spanish Rice Casserole

Serves 12   Serving Size 1 Cup
Fat Grams 3   Calories 154

Ingredients

1 cup	brown rice, uncooked
1 pkg.	kernel corn, frozen (16 oz.)
1 pkg.	Old El Paso taco seasoning mix
2 cans	tomato sauce (8 oz.)
2 cups	water
½ cup	onion, chopped
½ cup	green pepper
3 cups	ground chicken
½ cup	Bulgur wheat****
4	turkey bacon strips (microwave on high until crisp)

Preparation Instructions

Grind chicken in food processor. Microwave bacon on high until crist. Combine all ingredients. Pour into freezer bag and freeze.

When *thawed, cover and bake at 375° for 55 minutes.

Serve alone or over taco shells or tortillas (add one fat gram each).

Recipe Option

Serves 12   Serving Size 1 Cup
Fat Grams 6   Calories 179

In place of chicken try:

1½ cup	ground beef, extra lean
1 cup	bulgur wheat

* See section on **Thawing Instructions**
**** See Bulgur Wheat recipe in Recipe Basics section.

Menu Suggestions

Water	12 oz.
Veggie	refried beans, salad
Grain	corn torilla chips
Fruit	fresh fruit cup
Protein	**SPANISH RICE CASSEROLE**

Stroganoff

Serves 8
Fat Grams Beef 10
　　　　　Chicken 3

Serving Size 1 Cup
Calories Beef 244
　　　　　Chicken 176

Ingredients

2 cups	ground beef, extra lean
1 cup	bulgur wheat****
1 cup	onion
¼ tsp.	garlic, minced
¼ cup	whole wheat flour
½ tsp.	salt
¼ cup	pepper
1 cup	mushroom pieces (or 2, 4 oz. cans, drained)
1 can	Cream of Mushroom Soup**
	or
1 pkg.	stroganoff sauce mix***
1-1½ cups	skim milk
1 cup	nonfat sour cream (8 oz.)

* See section on **Thawing Instructions**
** Campbell's Healthy Request soup -10 1/2 oz
　　or See Recipe Basics section for recipe.
*** Possible MSG product. Read label.
**** See Bulgur Wheat recipe in Recipe Basics
　　　　section.

Preparation Instructions

Crack wheat in blender or food processor and boil for five minutes until tender.

Combine all ingredients. Pour into bag and freeze.

When *thawed, simmer uncovered for 15 minutes. Thin with skim milk if desired.

Serve over hot rice, baked potatoes or noodles.

Substitutions

In place of beef and bulgur wheat use:

3 cups　　chicken pieces

Menu Suggestions

Water	12 oz.
Veggie	mixed veggie salad
Grain	w.w. rolls
Fruit	sliced tomatoes
Protein	**BEEF STROGANOFF**

Stuffed Manicotti

Serves 7
Fat Grams 8

Serving Size 2 Manicotti Shells
Calories 423

Ingredients

Meat Sauce

3 cups	chicken pieces
1½ cups	water
4 tsp.	sweet basil
16 oz.	tomato sauce
½ cup	onion, chopped
1½ tsp.	salt
2 Tbl.	parsley, dry

Cheese Stuffing

12 oz.	nonfat ricotta cheese
12 oz.	nonfat cottage cheese
1	egg
1/3 cup	Parmesan cheese
2 Tbl.	parsley
¼ tsp.	salt
14	manicotti shells (8 oz.), uncooked
1 cup	Frigo Truly Lite skim mozzarella cheese (to be added at time of baking)
to taste	paprika

Preparation Instructions

Combine ingredients for cheese stuffing and fill dry shells. Put into freezer bag. Then combine ingredients for meat sauce and put in smaller freezer bag.

Cook this meal straight from frozen to done. Put frozen manicotti in a pan. Pour thawed sauce over manicotti. Cover and bake at 400° for one hour. Add one cup part skim mozzarella cheese, sprinkle with paprika for color and bake an additional 15 minutes uncovered.

Menu Suggestions

W$_{ater}$	12 oz.
V$_{eggie}$	corn-on-the-cob, garden salad
G$_{rain}$	w.w. rolls
F$_{ruit}$	sliced tomatoes
P$_{rotein}$	**MANICOTTI**

* See section on **Thawing Instructions**

Sweet and Sour Chicken

Serves 6　　　　Serving Size 1¼ Cup
Fat Grams 3　　　Calories 277

Ingredients

3 cups	chicken pieces
½ cup	cider vinegar
¼ cup	ketchup
½ cup	brown sugar
2 Tbl.	cornstarch
	or
3 Tbl.	ULTRA GEL®
1½ cups	green pepper, chopped
1 can	pineapple tidbits (15 oz.), drained - reserve juice

* See section on **Thawing Instructions**

Preparation Instructions

In about two teaspoons vegetable oil, saute green pepper until tender crisp. In a small bowl, combine vinegar, ketchup, brown sugar, pineapple juice and ULTRA GEL® or cornstarch. Add to green peppers and bring mixture to a boil if using cornstarch. If using ULTRA GEL® there's no need to heat. Stir until sauce thickens. Remove from heat and stir in pineapple and chicken. Bag and freeze.

When *thawed, heat through in saucepan or microwave and serve over brown rice.

Menu Suggestions

W$_{ater}$	12 oz.
V$_{eggie}$	steamed broccoli, veggie salad
G$_{rain}$	brown rice
F$_{ruit}$	broiled pinapple rounds
P$_{rotein}$	**SWEET AND SOUR CHICKEN**

Taco Pie

Serves 16   Serving Size 1/8 slice
Fat Grams 6   Calories 196

Ingredients

Hamburger Mixture

1 lb.	ground beef, extra lean (grind course)
1 can	pinto beans, mashed
1/2 cup	bulgur wheat****
1 med.	onion, chopped
2 cans	tomato sauce (8 oz.ea.)
1 Tbl.	chili powder

Dairy Mixture

1 cup	nonfat cottage cheese
1 can	Cream of Chicken Soup**
1 cup	skim milk

Topping

10	taco shells (1 FG ea.)
¼ cup	cheddar cheese, grated

Serve On

lettuce, shredded
corn
baked potato
rice

Fresh Toppings

to taste	green onion, chopped
to taste	tomatoes, chopped
to taste	tobasco / taco sauce

* See section on **Thawing Instructions**
** Campbell's Healthy Request soup 10 1/2 oz or see recipe in Recipe Basics section.

Preparation Instructions

Make hamburger mixture. Mix well. Spray two pie tins with nonstick cooking spray. Break three shells in half for each tin and spread them on the bottom. Spread meat mixture on top and add two broken taco shells on top of meat mixture. Blend cottage cheese, soup and milk together and spread over shells in pan. Sprinkle the top with grated cheese. Cover with foil and freeze.

Next day, remove from pans, place in freezer bags and return to freezer.

To prepare, spray original tins with cooking spray and put pies in tins. Bake covered from frozen to done for one hour at 400°.

Menu Suggestions

Water	12 oz.
Veggie	baked squash, salad
Grain	whole wheat roll
Fruit	fresh sliced tomatoes
Protein	**TACO CASSEROLE**

**** See Bulgur Wheat recipe in Recipe Basics section.

Tostadas

Serves 12   Serving Size 1 Tostada
Fat Grams 4   Calories 138

Ingredients

Filling

½ cup	ground beef, extra lean
½ cup	bulgur wheat,**** re-constituted
1 can	kidney beans, drained
1 can	vegetarian refried beans
½ cup	onion, chopped
½ cup	zucchini, grated
½ cup	carrots, grated

Other

12	corn tortilla
1 bottle	taco sauce
1 Tbl.	skim mozzarella cheese, per tostada

* See section on **Thawing Instructions**
**** See Bulgur Wheat recipe in Recipe Basics
section.

Preparation Instructions

Mix all filling ingredients together and seal in freezer bag. Freeze.

*Thaw, stir mixture and heat in microwave for four or five minutes or until hot clear through.

To serve, crisp tortillas in the oven for one to three minutes at 400° or on the range at medium heat for approximately three minutes. Spread two tablespoons filler on top of a corn taco shell. Top with fresh cut tomatoes, lettuce, sprinkle lightly with cheese.

Add hot sauce to taste and serve.

Menu Suggestions

Water   12 oz.
Veggie   sliced avacodo
Grain   taco shell
Fruit   sliced tomatoes
Protein **VEGGIE TOSTADAS**

Tuna Casserole

Serves 6
Fat Grams 4

Serving Size 1 cup
Calories 201

Ingredients

1 pkg.	wide egg noodles (12 oz.) OR homemade whole wheat noodles
1 can	Cream of Chicken soup**
1 can	Cream of Mushroom soup**
1 pkg.	peas, frozen (10 oz.) (optional)
1½ cups skim milk
1 can	tuna, drained (water-packed)

Preparation Instructions

Bring water to boil and cook noodles until almost done (five minutes), then combine all ingredients and put in freezer bag.

When *thawed, cover and bake at 350° for 50 minutes.

* See section on **Thawing Instructions**
** Campbell's Healthy Request soup -10 1/2 oz or see recipe in Recipe Basics section.

Menu Suggestions

W_{ater}	12 oz.
V_{eggie}	mixed veggie plate
G_{rain}	w.w. bread
F_{ruit}	cantaloupe
P_{rotein}	**TUNA CASSEROLE**

RECIPE BASICS
INDEX

81

RECIPE BASIC
BBQ Sauce

Batch: Makes 3 Cups
Fat Grams 2   Calories 357

Individual Portions:
Serves 12   Serving Size 2 oz.
Fat Grams = trace   Calories 30

½ cup	water
1 tsp.	fructose or honey
½ Tbl.	molasses
½ pkg.	Butter Buds
1/3 cup	lemon juice
1 Tbl.	Worcestershire sauce
1 cup	catsup
1 med.	onion, finely chopped
½ tsp.	pepper
1 tsp.	salt

Cook on high until boiling.

Use hot or cold. Freeze and *thaw as needed.

Serve over beef, turkey, chicken, etc.

* See section on **Thawing Instructions**

Brown Rice
Whole Grain

Makes 2 Cups   Serving Size 1/2 Cup
Fat Grams 1   Calories 116

2 cups   water
1 cup   brown rice

Bring two cups of water to boil. Add one cup rice and bring back to a boil. Lower the heat until the water is just bubbling. Turn heat as low as possible. Cover.

Cook 45 - 50 minutes. Turn off the heat, remove the lid and let stand five minutes to dry out.

Note

For greater quantities of rice, simply double the rice in proportion to the water amount.

Bread Crumbs
Whole Wheat

1 Slice Makes 1/2 Cup Bread Crumbs
Fat Grams 1   Calories 65

Fresh or Dried

Put fresh bread in food processor with the chopper blade. Process until bread is in fine pieces.

Use immediately or spread on cookie sheet and dry in 400° oven for five to ten minutes until completely dry and toasty.

Store crumbs in a freezer bag in the freezer for future use.

RECIPE BASIC
Bulgur Wheat
1 Cup Makes a Serving Size of 2 Cups
Fat Grams 3   Calories 600

1
Rinse whole wheat kernels in cool water. Discard water.

2
Add hot water until 1" above level of wheat. Bring water to boil (stir occasionally). Reduce heat to low and steam for 40 to 50 minutes or until water is absorbed into wheat.

NOTE
If you are going to use it right away, drain off any excess water and crack the wheat in a food processor after step 2. Dry any leftover wheat.

3
Spread wheat thinly on a cookie sheet and dry in the oven at 200 degrees, until very dry (approximately two hours).

4
When completely dry, it can be cracked in a blender, food processor, mill or stored as in (whole) in a container.

5
If the recipe calls for cooked bulgur, simply boil cracked wheat in water for 5 to 10 minutes, approximately doubling the volume. Pour off excess water and use.

Make a big pot full and store the leftovers for additional recipes.

RECIPE BASIC
Cheese Sauce
Servings 10.5   Serving Size 1/2 cup
Fat Grams 3   Calories 112

1 crtn.	nonfat cottage cheese (12 oz.)
1 can	skim evaporated milk (5 oz.)
½ cup	cheddar cheese, shredded
1 pkg.	Butter Buds
to taste	pepper, freshly ground
to taste	lite salt
2-4 Tbl.	ULTRA GEL.

Combine cottage cheese and milk in blender. Process until smooth. In small sauce-pan, heat mixture over me-dium low heat, stirring con-stantly. Add cheese, salt, pepper and Butter Buds. Stir until cheese melts. Thicken with Ultra Gel. For Color (optional) add three drops yellow food coloring and one drop red. Stir vigorously. Freeze.

*Thaw, serve over veg-gies, macaroni and cheese or nachos.

84

Cream Soup Base

Makes 3 cups   Serving Size 24 oz.
Fat Grams 1   Calories 562

Ingredients

2 cups	nonfat powdered milk
1 cup	ULTRA GEL.
2 Tbl.	dried onion flakes
½ tsp.	pepper
1 tsp.	thyme leaves
1 tsp.	basil leaves
to taste	lite salt (approx. 1 tsp.)

Mix all ingredients together well in a blender. Use as a base for all cream soups. This freezes well.

For Plain Cream Soup Add

1¼ cups	water

Cream soups may be used in recipes to replace canned, condensed soups. Water portions may be adjusted.

Cream of Celery Soup

Makes 2 Cups   Serving Size 16 oz.
Fat Grams 0   Calories 191

1/3 cup	Cream Soup Base
¼ cup	celery, pureed
1-1¼ cups	water

Cream of Chicken Soup

Makes 2 Cups   Serving Size 16 oz.
Fat Grams 0   Calories 212

1/3 cup	Cream Soup Base
1¼ cup	chicken broth***

Cream of Mushroom Soup

Makes 2 Cups   Serving Size 16 oz.
Fat Grams 0   Calories 197

1/3 cup	Cream Soup Base
1 can	mushrooms (4 oz.) finely chopped, save juice and add enough water to equal 1¼ cups liquid.

*** Possible MSG product. Read label.

Refried Beans

Makes 2 Cups
Fat Grams 1   Calories 472

Ingredients

1 can	pinto beans, drained
2 Tbl.	jalapeno pepper
2 Tbl.	green chilies
to taste	salt

Put in food processor and blend until smooth. Cook at high in microwave two to three minutes.

Serve in tacos, enchiladas, or as a side dish.

Tartar Sauce

Makes 1¼ Cup   Serving Size 1 Tbl.
Fat Grams 4   Calories 43

Ingredients

½ cup	mayonnaise
½ cup	plain nonfat yogurt
1 Tbl.	capers, drain, chop fine
2 Tbl.	dill pickle, chop fine
2 tsp.	lemon juice
1 tsp.	Dijon mustard
½ tsp.	onion, pureed or grated
1½ Tbl.	parsley, fresh chopped

RECIPE BASIC
Spaghetti Sauce

Makes 5 1/2 Cups
Fat Grams 1   Calories 570

2 sm. cans	tomato paste (6 oz.)
2 sm. cans	tomato sauce (7 3/4 oz.)
1 large can	tomato juice (12 oz.)
to taste	salt
to taste	thyme (appx. 1½ Tbl.)
1 large	onion, diced
2 tsp.	rosemary leaf
2 tsp.	oregano
½ tsp.	garlic powder
4 oz.	mushrooms, sliced, drained

Mix ingredients together in medium bowl. Cover and simmer for one to three hours. Refrigerate or freeze.

When *thawed, serve over spaghetti, chicken, turkey, potatoes, noodles, rice, etc.

* See section on **Thawing Instructions**

PERSONAL FAVORITE
RECIPE BASIC

88

PERSONAL FAVORITE
RECIPE BASIC

APPENDIX

89

Monthly Planning Sample

				WANT TO COOK FFR Page 80 **1**	FREEZER MEAL Chicken Poskets • Mike Piano 3:00 • Night Class **2**	FREEZER MEAL Ham Dinner • Date With Hubby **3**	WANT TO COOK FFR Page 99A **4**

WANT TO COOK FFR Page 98 **5**	FREEZER MEAL Chicken Lasagna • Family Night **6**	FREEZER MEAL Chicken Fajitas • Heather: Orthodontist 2:15 • Night Class **7**	FREEZER MEAL Ham Fried Rice • Office Party **8**	FREEZER MEAL Chicken Stir Fry • Mike Piano 3:00 • Night Class • Ldrshp. Mtg. 8 pm **9**	FREEZER MEAL BBQ Beef • Meet Michelle Shopping • Date With Hubby **10**	WANT TO COOK E&BL Page K-17 • Clint Concert 7:00 pm **11**

WANT TO COOK FFR Page 83 **12**	FREEZER MEAL Italian Chicken Casserole • Family Night **13**	FREEZER MEAL Halibut • Night Class **14**	FREEZER MEAL Chicken Enchiladas • 12:00 Lunch with Luana • Dentist 3:50 • Business Mtg. 8:00 pm **15**	FREEZER MEAL Chili • Mike Piano 3:00 • Night Class **16**	WANT TO COOK E&BL Page K-21 • Date With Hubby **17**	WANT TO COOK FFR Page 89 **18**

WANT TO COOK FFR Page 86B **19**	FREEZER MEAL Tostadas • Family Night **20**	FREEZER MEAL Party Time Turkey • Night Class **21**	WANT TO COOK FFR Page 87 • Carl's Boss Coming to Dinner **22**	FREEZER MEAL Shepard's Pie • Mike Piano 3:00 • Night Class **23**	FREEZER MEAL Chicken Noodle Soup • Date With Hubby **24**	WANT TO COOK FFR Page 86A **25**

WANT TO COOK FFR Page 82 **26**	FREEZER MEAL BBQ Chicken **MAIN COOKING DAYS** • Family Night	FREEZER MEAL Lasagna • Night Class	FREEZER MEAL Tuna Casserole • Meet with Lisa & Allan	FREEZER MEAL Citrus Chicken • Mike Piano 3:00 • Night Class **30**	FREEZER MEAL Fish and Herb Broil • Date with Hubby and Parents **31**	

• **E&BL = EAT & Be Lean®** manual • **FFR = EAT & Be Lean® FAVORITE FAMILY RECIPES** cookbook

Monthly Meal Planner

Make copies for each month. File along with the shopping list to be used for coming years.

• **E&BL = EAT** & Be Lean® manual • **FFR = EAT** & Be Lean® **FAVORITE FAMILY RECIPES** cookbook

Personalized

* Fat FREE
** No MSG

MEALS

1	_____	6	_____
2	_____	7	_____
3	_____	8	_____
4	_____	9	_____
5	_____	10	_____

VEGETABLES AND FRUITS

ITEM	SIZE / AMOUNT	# USED IN RECIPE	TOTAL	PRICE

DRYFOODS

ITEM	SIZE / AMOUNT	# USED IN RECIPE	TOTAL	PRICE

MEATS

ITEM	SIZE / AMOUNT	# USED IN RECIPE	TOTAL	PRICE

Equivalents: 1 lb. hamburger = 16 oz. = appx. 3 cups chunked
1 lb. boneless, skinless chicken = 16 oz. = appx. 2 1/2 cups chopped
1 boneless, skinless chicken breast = appx. 1 cup chopped
1 large onion = appx. 1 cup chopped

Shopping Planner

11 _____ 16 _____
12 _____ 17 _____
13 _____ 18 _____
14 _____ 19 _____
15 _____ 20 _____

CANNED FOODS

ITEM	SIZE / AMOUNT	# USED IN RECIPE	TOTAL	PRICE

FROZEN FOODS

ITEM	SIZE / AMOUNT	# USED IN RECIPE	TOTAL	PRICE

DAIRY SECTION

ITEM	SIZE / AMOUNT	# USED IN RECIPE	TOTAL	PRICE

Equivalents: | Total $
1 lb. cheese = appx. 4 cups grated
1 green pepper = appx. 1 cup chopped
2 medium carrots = appx. 1 cup shredded
2 stalks celery = appx. 1 cup chopped

EAT & Be Lean® SUCCESS SHEET®	DATE	TOTAL
	STUDENT	

BREAKFAST

	PLAN	AMOUNT OR CHANGES	FAT GRAMS	FIBER	SATISFACTION (7 - 8)
WATER	[ ]				
VEGGIE	[ ]				
GRAIN	[ ]				
FRUIT	[ ]				
PROTEIN	[ ]				
WATER	[ ]				
SNACK					

LUNCH

	PLAN	AMOUNT OR CHANGES	FAT GRAMS	FIBER	SATISFACTION (7 - 8)
WATER	[ ]				
VEGGIE	[ ]				
GRAIN	[ ]				
FRUIT	[ ]				
PROTEIN	[ ]				
WATER	[ ]				
SNACK					

DINNER

	PLAN	AMOUNT OR CHANGES	FAT GRAMS	FIBER	SATISFACTION (7 - 8)
WATER	[ ]				
VEGGIE	[ ]				
GRAIN	[ ]				
FRUIT	[ ]				
PROTEIN	[ ]				
WATER	[ ]				
SNACK					

TYPE OF PLANNED EXERCISE	MINUTES	PULSE	NOTE: PULSE should be 11-18 beats per 6 second count.	FIBER TOTALS	TOTAL FAT GRAMS
ACTUAL			EXERCISE for a 60 minute period and **burn double the fat the second 30 minutes.**	25 Grams Minimum	20 to 33 is ideal to start with

SCORING	CHECK	POINTS	ITEM	QUESTIONS - COMMENTS
	[ ]	+3	All boxes marked	
	[ ]	+2	Exercise goal met	
	[ ]	+2	Positive thinking marked **YES**	
	[ ]	+1	Fat grams added	
	[ ]	+1	Fiber recorded (optional bonus points)	
	[ ]	+1	Pulse recorded	
	[ ]	+1	Satisfaction level recorded	
	[ ]	+1	Almost all boxes marked	
	[ ]	- 1	Sweet snack / fat snack / pop	
	[ ]	- 2	Meal skipped	
	[ ]	- 2	Positive thinking marked **NO**	

TOTAL POINTS	POSITIVE THINKING I am practicing positive self-talk and repeating my affirmations throughout the day. [ ] YES [ ] NO

■ Success Sheets

Research indicates that meal skippers have a tendency to be fatter, have higher cholesterol levels and more insulin resistance, which leads to hypoglycemia, diabetes and worsening obesity. It's very important that you know how you are presently eating, exercising and thinking in order to change and see a difference. For this reason, we are introducing just enough information to enable you to become familiar with and start benefiting from the use of the Success Sheets.

If you will learn to plan ahead on your meals for the whole month, implementing the *Too Busy To Cook* techniques, using a Success Sheet will be simple and very helpful in changing your less healthy eating habits to better ones.

Below is a brief explanation on **how to use the sheet**. Later, you can reference the *EAT & Be Lean® SUCCESS FORMULA* manual for more detailed information on how it all works.

1. **Eat often** and always **to complete satisfaction**. Often is a minimum of three meals per day plus snacks on veggie, grain and fruit items. Locate the spaces on the Success Sheet that are provided for what you plan to eat and what you really end up eating. On the far right portion of the Success Sheet you will find a satisfaction box. Refer to the Satisfaction Chart below for scoring information.

2. **Balance** your eating. Every day you should have 4+ grains, 4+ vegetables, 3+ fruit and around 3 1/2 to 4 oz. of protein. Protein may be obtained in the form of lean meats or better yet, by mixing a whole grain with either beans, peas or lentils for a complete protein.

SATISFACTION CHART	
10	CALL IN PARAMEDICS (Over eating is stressful)
9	VERY UNCOMFORTABLE (The "Pumpkin pie did me in...")
8	SLIGHTLY OVERFULL ⎤ (PERFECT - High energy,
7	COMPLETELY SATISFIED ⎦ Lowers fat setpoint)
6	SATISFIED
5	FENCE SITTING (No Signals)
4	GRUMBLING A LITTLE (Snack on veggies, grains & fruits)
3	HEARTY APPETITE (Eat NOW!)
2	REALLY FAMISHED (Weak: Blood sugar too low!)
1	STARVED (Faint, no hunger, numb)

3. **Fat** is important for health and fat loss. Yes, fat loss! Stay between 20 and 33 grams of fat per day to begin with. As your calories increase naturally, remember to raise the fat grams to stay within a 15% to 20% range of fat in the form of calories to ensure proper health and energy levels.

4. Note the **exercise** section near the bottom of the sheet. Moderate aerobic exercise should be performed three to six days per week for 30 to 60 minutes each session. Vary the exercises to maintain interest and always remember to be moderate. Working around 65% of your maximum is the best percentage for fat burning. Using the 6-Second Pulse Chart will help you find the proper exercise level for you.

6-SECOND PULSE CHART		
Age	**65% of Maximum**	**6-Second Count**
10 - 20	130	13 - 18
20 - 30	124	12 - 17
30 - 40	117	12 - 16
40 - 50	111	11 - 15
50 - 60	104	10 - 15
60 - 70	98	10 - 14
80 - 90	85	9 - 12
90 - 100	78	8 - 11

Take your pulse with two fingers (not your thumb) placed on the side of your neck to the right or left of your Adam's Apple for six seconds. Multiply the number by 10 for your workout pulse.

5. **Fiber** is figured in the box to the right of the fat grams. Your fiber intake should be no less than 25 grams per day. The more fiber in your diet, the better.

6. **Positive thinking** is very important, and like exercising, it releases endorphins which reduce the stress in your body and mind. Practice this daily. Check Yes or No accordingly to help you become more attentive to this essential part of good health.

Now total your **points** for the day. A perfect score is eleven. The closer you stay around eleven, the better you will feel and the faster you will see success.

For **in-depth information** on total health principles and simplifying the fat loss process, refer to the EAT & Be Lean SUCCESS FORMULA manual and nine week audio course. Refer to the product section in the back of the book for a description of the manual and other related products.

C Continued

D

E

F

G

H

H Continued

I

J

L

L Continued

M

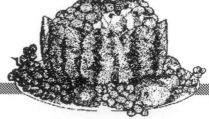

Recipe Index

▓ Products ▓

EAT & Be Lean. SUCCESS FORMULA Manual

The EAT & Be Lean book is a practical and easy to understand manual for learning the principles needed to obtain optimum health and leanness. This is a program that the entire family will benefit from regardless of age or condition. The principles are the same whether overweight, underweight or just the right weight, young or old. You'll learn why diets only make you fatter. You'll understand the importance of eating to complete satisfaction on the proper balance of foods, three to six times per day. You'll receive two months of menu plans, quick recipes and shopping lists that make it easy for you to implement the program into your regular daily routine. You'll discover the power of the "Three Part Formula for Success" that greatly speeds your progress towards permanent leanness and allows you to get on with the rest of your life. You'll learn that sweets are not forbidden when eaten at the appropriate time and find that your body becomes forgiving when you splurge.

EAT & Be Lean
Audio Cassette Course

The nine week audio course has eight audio cassette tapes (one hour each) that provide the nine sessions of instruction. Additional information and explanations that are provided by the audio course provides an ideal companion to the SUCCESS FORMULA manual. Studies indicate that once you hear, see and write information down, you absorb approximately 13%. By listening over and over again, eventually you'll increase the 13% to 90% or 100% retention of sound, lean truths. The tapes make a great addition to your home library of learning.

AEROBIC-TIPS Aerobics Video

Aerobic-TIPS is a one hour low-impact aerobics video that opens a whole new approach to aerobic dance. It is designed specifically for the EAT & Be Lean program and is a unique, enjoyable and efficient way to burn fat. It offers a triple bonus to participants: One, it has two complete programs of 30 and 60 minutes that are great for all ages. Two, throughout the exercise routines, the EAT & Be Lean principles and sound exercise techniques are continuously being reinforced. Three, positive subliminal messages are continuously reinforcing the same principles and encouraging you while you exercise. Participants are all family members ranging in age from 11 to 88.

AEROBIKIDS Aerobics Video

Aerobikids is a low-impact video that is currently being used in elementary school fitness programs throughout the United States and Canada as well as by individuals in their own homes. The aerobics are safe, fun and great for kids and  adults. The tape contains a 15 and 25 minute program including a pre-warm up, stretch out, pre-cardio, aerobic workout, walking cool down and final flexibility. Simplified diet information on the subject of anorexia, bulimia and nutrition principles add the finishing touch.

WALKING WORKOUT

This one hour audio cassette program is filled with fun, motivating music and subliminal messages that continually reinforce the same principles taught in the classes. Positive messages such as "Success is a way of life for me" and "I am a naturally lean person", encourage a happier, healthier, leaner you. It has a warm-up aerobic pace, fast training pace and cool down music that makes it fun to exercise. Since the music matches the Aerobic-TIPS video music selections, you will be able to conveniently take the Walking Workout audio cassette tape with you on vacations and perform the aerobics program you've learned through the video at home.

EAT & Be Lean Success Story Audio Cassettes
Tape #1 or #2

EAT & Be Lean realizes your need for encouraging words from others who have proven the program to be successful in their own lives. There may be many experiences similar to your own that you will be able to relate to.

Each audio cassette contains several personal stories of people who call in voluntarily to express their appreciation for the wonderful changes that are taking place in their lives and the lives of their families. They share their successes without solicitation because they are interested in helping others to find the same happiness they are experiencing.

It's helpful to have the support from others to maintain the positive attitude necessary to get through the time it takes to make permanent changes. These stories will touch your heart as you get to know the individuals sharing them.

EAT & Be Lean SEMINAR VIDEO (1 hour)

Chris Thornock presents an overview of the EAT & Be Lean program that will be effective in helping you understand the basic principles of good health and permanent leanness. It provides additional motivation to start you on the road to educating yourself, your family or whom ever you choose to share the program with.

EAT & Be Lean FAVORITE FAMILY RECIPES Cookbook

Over 250 delicious recipes that assist you and your family in making the transition from a high fat, high sugar diet to a healthier level of low-fat, low-sugar recipes. The book offers four weeks of new menu plans with shopping lists along with individual meal plans on each Main Dish recipe. It also includes an ingredients index, recipe healthification section, first choice ingredients section on health and nutrition basics.

EVENING PRIMROSE OIL

Evening Primrose Oil is a wonderful, natural source of essential oils that produce a myriad of health benefits to the body. One of the benefits is that it assists the body in its normal process of eliminating excess fat. For the highly resistant individuals it can assist in regenerating your system without causing undesirable side affects that diet gimmicks bring on. Count one fat gram into your daily intake for every three gel capsules you take. Take one to two capsules per meal.

THE COMPLETE FAT BOOK
By Karen J. Bellerson

This book contains 504 pages with over 25,000 foods listing fat grams, percent fat and calorie information. THE COMPLETE FAT BOOK is an inexpensive, valuable tool for you to use in your quest towards permanent leanness. The book is small enough to carry in your pocket or purse and provides detailed information on national brands, fast food items, health foods, homemade recipes, frozen entrees and more.

The Quest for Love & Self-Esteem
by Virginia Bourgeous

80 pages explain that everyone wants to be loved and appreciated. The author discusses why people feel unloved and explains many methods used to satisfy emotional needs. Interesting case studies depict unsuccessful ways people try to gain love and self-esteem with types such as the perfectionist, the know-it-all, the dictator, the martyr, the nomad, the hypochondriac, and the loner described.

In Bad Taste, The M.S.G. Syndrome
by Schwartz and Coleman

MSG (Monosodium Glutamate) is a universally used flavor enhancer that can cause mild to severe headaches, dizziness, shortness of breath, heart irregularities, asthma, gas and bloating and serious depression. This comprehensive, first-of-its-kind study dares to explore the dangers of this potentially harmful substance found in many packaged, processed and frozen foods. These foods are served to you in the finest restaurants and to our children in school.

This book teaches you how to recognize the symptoms of MSG-sensitivity, ways to shop smart, how to spot misleading labeling and much more.

Set For Life - Recipe Book
By Jane Merrill and Karen Sunderland

Now in its fourth printing, newly revised and enlarged Set For Life features more than 350 tasty low-fat, low-sugar recipes that help you make the life-style changes you want. These delicious family favorites are unbelievably easy and fast to prepare. In addition, Set For Life combines the positive, highly motivating, easy-to-read style of its authors with the latest research on weight control. Order your copy of this best-seller, and do what its pages outline. Before you know it, you'll realize what the cover promises: you'll eat more...weigh less...and feel terrific.

ULTRA GEL®
Carnet, Inc.

ULTRA GEL® is a modified food starch made from waxy maize (corn). It is used in many types of foods because it quickly thickens cold or hot liquids. Products made with ULTRA GEL® can be refrigerated or frozen and reheated successfully. Gravies and sauces can be made truly "fat free" and good quality reduced-fat baked products are possible. Jams, fruit spreads, syrups and fruit glazes can be made with little or no added sugar; and bestof all, you are in control of artificial flavorings, colorings, and other additives. ULTRA GEL® is also fool-proof, as the consistency can be easily adjusted with the addition of slightly more ULTRA GEL® or liquid.

Nine Week SUPPORT GROUP PACKET

The support group packet provides valuable lesson plan information, sample handouts, roll cards and other information needed to start a support group in your area. The best results are obtained by working with other people in a support group effort. It is fun and exciting to see the successes of each other as you work together. Order your support group packet today and join in the fun.

A support group is simple to start and gathers new students rapidly from your community. They are fun, helpful and motivational to each person in atten-dance. Support group packets are available for $4.00. For more information on how to get in contact with any of the over 250 support groups throughout the world or to order your support group packet, contact EAT & Be Lean by phone or mail.

Product Order Form

How did you hear about us?
Friend   [ ]   Newspaper [ ]   Radio [ ]   Other:
Television [ ]   Magazine   [ ]   Store [ ]   _____

Name _____

Address_____

City _____County _____

State _____ Zip _____Phone _____

No.	Product Description	Price	Shipping	Total
	Too Busy To Cook - Technique / Cookbook	9.95	+ 1.05	
	FAVORITE FAMILY RECIPES Cookbook	11.95	+ 1.05	
	EAT & Be Lean SUCCESS FORMULA Book	12.95	+ 1.48	
	Nine Week Audio Cassette Course	49.95	+ 1.91	
	AEROBIC-TIPS Video - 30 & 60 Minutes	19.95	+ 1.05	
	AEROBIKIDS Video - 15 & 30 Minutes	14.95	+ 1.05	
	Set For Life - Cookbook	16.95	+ 1.48	
	WALKING WORKOUT Audio Cassette	9.95	+ .75	
	Success Stories Audio - 1 or 2	4.95	+ .75	
	Seminar Video - 1 Hour Presentation	9.95	+ 1.05	
	Quest for Love and Self Esteem	6.95	+ 1.05	
	The complete FAT Book - Food Reference	6.00	+ 1.05	
	In Bad Taste - MSG Book	4.99	+ 1.05	
	ULTRA GEL® - (Thickener) 2 lb. container	8.95	+ Call	
	Evening Primrose Oil (EPO) capsules	15.95	+ 1.21	
	Subtotal			
	Utah Residents Add 6.25% Sales Tax			
	Grand Total			

VISA	Mastercard	DISCOVER	CHECK #	CASH $

Card # _____ Exp. Date _____

Authorized Signature _____

FOR OFFICE USE ONLY	ORDER DATE
CLERK	DATE FILLED

THORNOCK INTERNATIONAL PRODUCTIONS, INC. • P.O. Box 1132 • Clearfield, UT 84015 • 801-776-1176

Product Order Form

Name _____

Address_____

City _____County _____

State _____ Zip _____ Phone _____

No.	Product Description	Price Shipping	Total
	Too Busy To Cook - Technique / Cookbook	9.95 + 1.05	
	FAVORITE FAMILY RECIPES Cookbook	11.95 + 1.05	
	EAT & Be Lean SUCCESS FORMULA Book	12.95 + 1.48	
	Nine Week Audio Cassette Course	49.95 + 1.91	
	AEROBIC-TIPS Video - 30 & 60 Minutes	19.95 + 1.05	
	AEROBIKIDS Video - 15 & 30 Minutes	14.95 + 1.05	
	Set For Life - Cookbook	16.95 + 1.48	
	WALKING WORKOUT Audio Cassette	9.95 + .75	
	Success Stories Audio - 1 or 2	4.95 + .75	
	Seminar Video - 1 Hour Presentation	9.95 + 1.05	
	Quest for Love and Self Esteem	6.95 + 1.05	
	The complete FAT Book - Food Reference	6.00 + 1.05	
	In Bad Taste - MSG Book	4.99 + 1.05	
	ULTRA GEL® - (Thickener) 2 lb. container	8.95 + Call	
	Evening Primrose Oil (EPO) capsules	15.95 + 1.21	
	Subtotal		
	Utah Residents Add 6.25% Sales Tax		
	Grand Total		

VISA	Mastercard	DISCOVER	CHECK #	CASH $

Card #   Exp. Date

Authorized Signature

FOR OFFICE USE ONLY	ORDER DATE
CLERK	DATE FILLED

THORNOCK INTERNATIONAL PRODUCTIONS, INC. • P.O. Box 1132 • Clearfield, UT 84015 • 801-776-1176